# THE REALLY SIMPLE

# 365

# ONE YEAR
# WALKING
# CHALLENGE

## 'MAKE WALKING A HEALTHY HABIT'

## Disclaimer

# BENEFITS OF WALKING

- Increases heart and lung fitness

- Reduces the risk of heart disease and stroke

- Helps control conditions such as high blood pressure, high cholesterol, joint and muscular pain or stiffness, and diabetes

- Creates stronger bones and improved balance

- Increases muscle strength and endurance

- Controls body fat & helps to reduce weight

## Ideally...

- Increase walking distance slightly each week

- Build up to a faster than normal pace and maintain

- Gently stretch leg muscles for a few minutes before setting off

- Take water along for hydration

- Wear loose clothing

- Wear shoes or boots that reflect your route

## Try to...

- Vary your walks each day/week

- Develop the habit of walking every day

- Log any little injuries that may occur

- If you struggle to make time for a walk every day, just have a 5-minute blast around the block and log it!

- Try not to break the habit. Log even the shortest of walks if you are stuck for time.

- Enjoy every journey!

# HOW TO USE YOUR WALKING LOG

This logbook is all about simplicity. There is no need to jot down every little detail of your walks, just the main things that will get you to a healthier and happier place!

According to a European Social Journal study, it can take 18 days for a habit to form and up to an average of 66 days for the habit to become an automatic behaviour.

Once this is achieved, it's plain sailing! So don't get disheartened if the first 3 weeks seem to be a bit of a struggle. It gets easier.

Once you're up and ~~running~~ walking the 365-day challenge, you will find it hard to miss a day and that's when walking becomes a really fun and healthy exercise that benefits you now, & long term.

Start this journey slowly… no need to rush this challenge, it will all come together. Simply write down the date, a brief description of your walking route, note the start and end time as well as the distance walked. If you have a smartwatch or a pedometer, you can also note the average pace achieved per mile. (This acts as great motivation for future walks)

Don't forget to also jot down any little niggles or injuries you pick up. (This helps you to understand where to place those plasters and band-aids when breaking in new footwear!)

Most importantly, enjoy the journey, take in the air, and make the most of your new healthy habit!

## Example

| Day/Date | Brief Route Info | | Walk No. 001 |
|---|---|---|---|
| Sun 30 May | Newtown Lane, Trafford Road, Tagwell Road | | |
| **Time Start** | **Time Walking** | **Distance** | **Avg Pace/Mile** |
| 12.10pm | 52 mins | 3.08 miles | 16.59 |
| **Aches , Pains & Notes** | | | |
| Blister started under big toe on right foot. Left shin a little sore. Weather - fine and sunny. | | | |

# 365 DAY WALKING CHALLENGE - WEEK 1

| Day/Date | Brief Route Info | | Walk No. 001 |
|---|---|---|---|
| | | | |
| Time Start | Time Walking | Distance | Avg Pace/Mile |
| | | | |
| Aches , Pains & Notes | | | |
| | | | |

| Day/Date | Brief Route Info | | Walk No. 002 |
|---|---|---|---|
| | | | |
| Time Start | Time Walking | Distance | Avg Pace/Mile |
| | | | |
| Aches , Pains & Notes | | | |
| | | | |

| Day/Date | Brief Route Info | | Walk No. 003 |
|---|---|---|---|
| | | | |
| Time Start | Time Walking | Distance | Avg Pace/Mile |
| | | | |
| Aches , Pains & Notes | | | |
| | | | |

| Day/Date | Brief Route Info | | Walk No. 004 |
|---|---|---|---|
| | | | |
| Time Start | Time Walking | Distance | Avg Pace/Mile |
| | | | |
| Aches , Pains & Notes | | | |
| | | | |

| Day/Date | Brief Route Info | | Walk No. 005 |
|---|---|---|---|
| | | | |

| Time Start | Time Walking | Distance | Avg Pace/Mile |
|---|---|---|---|
| | | | |

**Aches , Pains & Notes**

| Day/Date | Brief Route Info | | Walk No. 006 |
|---|---|---|---|
| | | | |

| Time Start | Time Walking | Distance | Avg Pace/Mile |
|---|---|---|---|
| | | | |

**Aches , Pains & Notes**

| Day/Date | Brief Route Info | | Walk No. 007 |
|---|---|---|---|
| | | | |

| Time Start | Time Walking | Distance | Avg Pace/Mile |
|---|---|---|---|
| | | | |

**Aches , Pains & Notes**

# SUMMARY

| Time Walking | Distance Walked | Average Pace |
|---|---|---|
| | | |

| Start Weight | Weight Now | + /- |
|---|---|---|
| | | |

# 365 DAY WALKING CHALLENGE - WEEK 2

| Day/Date | Brief Route Info | | Walk No. 008 |
|---|---|---|---|
| | | | |

| Time Start | Time Walking | Distance | Avg Pace/Mile |
|---|---|---|---|
| | | | |

| Aches , Pains & Notes | | | |
|---|---|---|---|
| | | | |

| Day/Date | Brief Route Info | | Walk No. 009 |
|---|---|---|---|
| | | | |

| Time Start | Time Walking | Distance | Avg Pace/Mile |
|---|---|---|---|
| | | | |

| Aches , Pains & Notes | | | |
|---|---|---|---|
| | | | |

| Day/Date | Brief Route Info | | Walk No. 010 |
|---|---|---|---|
| | | | |

| Time Start | Time Walking | Distance | Avg Pace/Mile |
|---|---|---|---|
| | | | |

| Aches , Pains & Notes | | | |
|---|---|---|---|
| | | | |

| Day/Date | Brief Route Info | | Walk No. 011 |
|---|---|---|---|
| | | | |

| Time Start | Time Walking | Distance | Avg Pace/Mile |
|---|---|---|---|
| | | | |

| Aches , Pains & Notes | | | |
|---|---|---|---|
| | | | |

| Day/Date | Brief Route Info | | Walk No. 012 |
|---|---|---|---|
| | Time Start | Time Walking | Distance | Avg Pace/Mile |

| Time Start | Time Walking | Distance | Avg Pace/Mile |
|---|---|---|---|
| | | | |

**Aches , Pains & Notes**

| Day/Date | Brief Route Info | | Walk No. 013 |
|---|---|---|---|

| Time Start | Time Walking | Distance | Avg Pace/Mile |
|---|---|---|---|
| | | | |

**Aches , Pains & Notes**

| Day/Date | Brief Route Info | | Walk No. 014 |
|---|---|---|---|

| Time Start | Time Walking | Distance | Avg Pace/Mile |
|---|---|---|---|
| | | | |

**Aches , Pains & Notes**

# SUMMARY

| Time Walking | Distance Walked | Average Pace |
|---|---|---|
| | | |

| Start Weight | Weight Now | + /- |
|---|---|---|
| | | |

# 365 DAY WALKING CHALLENGE - WEEK 3

| Day/Date | Brief Route Info | | Walk No. 015 |
|---|---|---|---|
| **Time Start** | **Time Walking** | **Distance** | **Avg Pace/Mile** |
| | | | |

**Aches , Pains & Notes**

| Day/Date | Brief Route Info | | Walk No. 016 |
|---|---|---|---|
| **Time Start** | **Time Walking** | **Distance** | **Avg Pace/Mile** |
| | | | |

**Aches , Pains & Notes**

| Day/Date | Brief Route Info | | Walk No. 017 |
|---|---|---|---|
| **Time Start** | **Time Walking** | **Distance** | **Avg Pace/Mile** |
| | | | |

**Aches , Pains & Notes**

| Day/Date | Brief Route Info | | Walk No. 018 |
|---|---|---|---|
| **Time Start** | **Time Walking** | **Distance** | **Avg Pace/Mile** |
| | | | |

**Aches , Pains & Notes**

| Day/Date | Brief Route Info | | Walk No. 019 |
|---|---|---|---|
| | | | |

| Time Start | Time Walking | Distance | Avg Pace/Mile |
|---|---|---|---|
| | | | |

**Aches , Pains & Notes**

| |
|---|
| |

| Day/Date | Brief Route Info | | Walk No. 020 |
|---|---|---|---|
| | | | |

| Time Start | Time Walking | Distance | Avg Pace/Mile |
|---|---|---|---|
| | | | |

**Aches , Pains & Notes**

| |
|---|
| |

| Day/Date | Brief Route Info | | Walk No. 021 |
|---|---|---|---|
| | | | |

| Time Start | Time Walking | Distance | Avg Pace/Mile |
|---|---|---|---|
| | | | |

**Aches , Pains & Notes**

| |
|---|
| |

# SUMMARY

| Time Walking | Distance Walked | Average Pace |
|---|---|---|
| | | |

| Start Weight | Weight Now | + /- |
|---|---|---|
| | | |

# 365 DAY WALKING CHALLENGE - WEEK 4

| Day/Date | Brief Route Info | | Walk No. 022 |
|---|---|---|---|
| | | | |

| Time Start | Time Walking | Distance | Avg Pace/Mile |
|---|---|---|---|
| | | | |

**Aches , Pains & Notes**



| Day/Date | Brief Route Info | | Walk No. 023 |
|---|---|---|---|
| | | | |

| Time Start | Time Walking | Distance | Avg Pace/Mile |
|---|---|---|---|
| | | | |

**Aches , Pains & Notes**



| Day/Date | Brief Route Info | | Walk No. 024 |
|---|---|---|---|
| | | | |

| Time Start | Time Walking | Distance | Avg Pace/Mile |
|---|---|---|---|
| | | | |

**Aches , Pains & Notes**



| Day/Date | Brief Route Info | | Walk No. 025 |
|---|---|---|---|
| | | | |

| Time Start | Time Walking | Distance | Avg Pace/Mile |
|---|---|---|---|
| | | | |

**Aches , Pains & Notes**

| Day/Date | Brief Route Info | | Walk No. 026 |
|---|---|---|---|
| | | | |

| Time Start | Time Walking | Distance | Avg Pace/Mile |
|---|---|---|---|
| | | | |

**Aches , Pains & Notes**

| | |
|---|---|
| | |

| Day/Date | Brief Route Info | | Walk No. 027 |
|---|---|---|---|
| | | | |

| Time Start | Time Walking | Distance | Avg Pace/Mile |
|---|---|---|---|
| | | | |

**Aches , Pains & Notes**

| | |
|---|---|
| | |

| Day/Date | Brief Route Info | | Walk No. 028 |
|---|---|---|---|
| | | | |

| Time Start | Time Walking | Distance | Avg Pace/Mile |
|---|---|---|---|
| | | | |

**Aches , Pains & Notes**

| | |
|---|---|
| | |

# SUMMARY

| Time Walking | Distance Walked | Average Pace |
|---|---|---|
| | | |

| Start Weight | Weight Now | + /- |
|---|---|---|
| | | |

# 365 DAY WALKING CHALLENGE - WEEK 5

| Day/Date | Brief Route Info | | Walk No. 029 |
|---|---|---|---|
| Time Start | Time Walking | Distance | Avg Pace/Mile |
| | | | |

**Aches , Pains & Notes**

| Day/Date | Brief Route Info | | Walk No. 030 |
|---|---|---|---|
| Time Start | Time Walking | Distance | Avg Pace/Mile |
| | | | |

**Aches , Pains & Notes**

| Day/Date | Brief Route Info | | Walk No. 031 |
|---|---|---|---|
| Time Start | Time Walking | Distance | Avg Pace/Mile |
| | | | |

**Aches , Pains & Notes**

| Day/Date | Brief Route Info | | Walk No. 032 |
|---|---|---|---|
| Time Start | Time Walking | Distance | Avg Pace/Mile |
| | | | |

**Aches , Pains & Notes**

| Day/Date | Brief Route Info | | Walk No. 033 |
|---|---|---|---|
| | | | |

| Time Start | Time Walking | Distance | Avg Pace/Mile |
|---|---|---|---|
| | | | |

**Aches , Pains & Notes**

| |
|---|
| |

| Day/Date | Brief Route Info | | Walk No. 034 |
|---|---|---|---|
| | | | |

| Time Start | Time Walking | Distance | Avg Pace/Mile |
|---|---|---|---|
| | | | |

**Aches , Pains & Notes**

| |
|---|
| |

| Day/Date | Brief Route Info | | Walk No. 035 |
|---|---|---|---|
| | | | |

| Time Start | Time Walking | Distance | Avg Pace/Mile |
|---|---|---|---|
| | | | |

**Aches , Pains & Notes**

| |
|---|
| |

# SUMMARY

| Time Walking | Distance Walked | Average Pace |
|---|---|---|
| | | |

| Start Weight | Weight Now | + /- |
|---|---|---|
| | | |

# 365 DAY WALKING CHALLENGE - WEEK 6

| Day/Date | Brief Route Info | | Walk No. 036 |
|---|---|---|---|
| | | | |
| Time Start | Time Walking | Distance | Avg Pace/Mile |
| | | | |

**Aches , Pains & Notes**

| Day/Date | Brief Route Info | | Walk No. 037 |
|---|---|---|---|
| | | | |
| Time Start | Time Walking | Distance | Avg Pace/Mile |
| | | | |

**Aches , Pains & Notes**

| Day/Date | Brief Route Info | | Walk No. 038 |
|---|---|---|---|
| | | | |
| Time Start | Time Walking | Distance | Avg Pace/Mile |
| | | | |

**Aches , Pains & Notes**

| Day/Date | Brief Route Info | | Walk No. 039 |
|---|---|---|---|
| | | | |
| Time Start | Time Walking | Distance | Avg Pace/Mile |
| | | | |

**Aches , Pains & Notes**

| Day/Date | Brief Route Info | | Walk No. 040 |
|---|---|---|---|
| | | | |

| Time Start | Time Walking | Distance | Avg Pace/Mile |
|---|---|---|---|
| | | | |

**Aches , Pains & Notes**

| | | | |
|---|---|---|---|
| | | | |

| Day/Date | Brief Route Info | | Walk No. 041 |
|---|---|---|---|
| | | | |

| Time Start | Time Walking | Distance | Avg Pace/Mile |
|---|---|---|---|
| | | | |

**Aches , Pains & Notes**

| | | | |
|---|---|---|---|
| | | | |

| Day/Date | Brief Route Info | | Walk No. 042 |
|---|---|---|---|
| | | | |

| Time Start | Time Walking | Distance | Avg Pace/Mile |
|---|---|---|---|
| | | | |

**Aches , Pains & Notes**

| | | | |
|---|---|---|---|
| | | | |

# SUMMARY

| Time Walking | Distance Walked | Average Pace |
|---|---|---|
| | | |

| Start Weight | Weight Now | + /- |
|---|---|---|
| | | |

# 365 DAY WALKING CHALLENGE - WEEK 7

| Day/Date | Brief Route Info | | Walk No. 043 |
|---|---|---|---|
| | | | |
| Time Start | Time Walking | Distance | Avg Pace/Mile |
| | | | |
| Aches , Pains & Notes | | | |
| | | | |

| Day/Date | Brief Route Info | | Walk No. 044 |
|---|---|---|---|
| | | | |
| Time Start | Time Walking | Distance | Avg Pace/Mile |
| | | | |
| Aches , Pains & Notes | | | |
| | | | |

| Day/Date | Brief Route Info | | Walk No. 045 |
|---|---|---|---|
| | | | |
| Time Start | Time Walking | Distance | Avg Pace/Mile |
| | | | |
| Aches , Pains & Notes | | | |
| | | | |

| Day/Date | Brief Route Info | | Walk No. 046 |
|---|---|---|---|
| | | | |
| Time Start | Time Walking | Distance | Avg Pace/Mile |
| | | | |
| Aches , Pains & Notes | | | |
| | | | |

| Day/Date | Brief Route Info | | Walk No. 047 |
|---|---|---|---|

| Time Start | Time Walking | Distance | Avg Pace/Mile |
|---|---|---|---|
| | | | |

**Aches , Pains & Notes**

| Day/Date | Brief Route Info | | Walk No. 048 |
|---|---|---|---|

| Time Start | Time Walking | Distance | Avg Pace/Mile |
|---|---|---|---|
| | | | |

**Aches , Pains & Notes**

| Day/Date | Brief Route Info | | Walk No. 049 |
|---|---|---|---|

| Time Start | Time Walking | Distance | Avg Pace/Mile |
|---|---|---|---|
| | | | |

**Aches , Pains & Notes**

# SUMMARY

| Time Walking | Distance Walked | Average Pace |
|---|---|---|
| | | |

| Start Weight | Weight Now | + /- |
|---|---|---|
| | | |

# 365 DAY WALKING CHALLENGE - WEEK 8

| Day/Date | Brief Route Info | | Walk No. 050 |
|---|---|---|---|
| | | | |
| Time Start | Time Walking | Distance | Avg Pace/Mile |
| | | | |

### Aches , Pains & Notes

| Day/Date | Brief Route Info | | Walk No. 051 |
|---|---|---|---|
| | | | |
| Time Start | Time Walking | Distance | Avg Pace/Mile |
| | | | |

### Aches , Pains & Notes

| Day/Date | Brief Route Info | | Walk No. 052 |
|---|---|---|---|
| | | | |
| Time Start | Time Walking | Distance | Avg Pace/Mile |
| | | | |

### Aches , Pains & Notes

| Day/Date | Brief Route Info | | Walk No. 053 |
|---|---|---|---|
| | | | |
| Time Start | Time Walking | Distance | Avg Pace/Mile |
| | | | |

### Aches , Pains & Notes

| Day/Date | Brief Route Info | | Walk No. 054 |
|---|---|---|---|
| | | | |

| Time Start | Time Walking | Distance | Avg Pace/Mile |
|---|---|---|---|
| | | | |

**Aches , Pains & Notes**

| | | | |
|---|---|---|---|
| | | | |

| Day/Date | Brief Route Info | | Walk No. 055 |
|---|---|---|---|
| | | | |

| Time Start | Time Walking | Distance | Avg Pace/Mile |
|---|---|---|---|
| | | | |

**Aches , Pains & Notes**

| | | | |
|---|---|---|---|
| | | | |

| Day/Date | Brief Route Info | | Walk No. 056 |
|---|---|---|---|
| | | | |

| Time Start | Time Walking | Distance | Avg Pace/Mile |
|---|---|---|---|
| | | | |

**Aches , Pains & Notes**

| | | | |
|---|---|---|---|
| | | | |

# SUMMARY

| Time Walking | Distance Walked | Average Pace |
|---|---|---|
| | | |

| Start Weight | Weight Now | + /- |
|---|---|---|
| | | |

# 365 DAY WALKING CHALLENGE – WEEK 9

| Day/Date | Brief Route Info | | Walk No. 057 |
|---|---|---|---|
| | | | |

| Time Start | Time Walking | Distance | Avg Pace/Mile |
|---|---|---|---|
| | | | |

**Aches , Pains & Notes**

| | | | |
|---|---|---|---|

| Day/Date | Brief Route Info | | Walk No. 058 |
|---|---|---|---|
| | | | |

| Time Start | Time Walking | Distance | Avg Pace/Mile |
|---|---|---|---|
| | | | |

**Aches , Pains & Notes**

| | | | |
|---|---|---|---|

| Day/Date | Brief Route Info | | Walk No. 059 |
|---|---|---|---|
| | | | |

| Time Start | Time Walking | Distance | Avg Pace/Mile |
|---|---|---|---|
| | | | |

**Aches , Pains & Notes**

| | | | |
|---|---|---|---|

| Day/Date | Brief Route Info | | Walk No. 060 |
|---|---|---|---|
| | | | |

| Time Start | Time Walking | Distance | Avg Pace/Mile |
|---|---|---|---|
| | | | |

**Aches , Pains & Notes**

| | | | |
|---|---|---|---|

| Day/Date | Brief Route Info | | Walk No. 061 |
|---|---|---|---|
| | | | |

| Time Start | Time Walking | Distance | Avg Pace/Mile |
|---|---|---|---|
| | | | |

**Aches , Pains & Notes**

| |
|---|
| |

| Day/Date | Brief Route Info | | Walk No. 062 |
|---|---|---|---|
| | | | |

| Time Start | Time Walking | Distance | Avg Pace/Mile |
|---|---|---|---|
| | | | |

**Aches , Pains & Notes**

| |
|---|
| |

| Day/Date | Brief Route Info | | Walk No. 063 |
|---|---|---|---|
| | | | |

| Time Start | Time Walking | Distance | Avg Pace/Mile |
|---|---|---|---|
| | | | |

**Aches , Pains & Notes**

| |
|---|
| |

# SUMMARY

| Time Walking | Distance Walked | Average Pace |
|---|---|---|
| | | |

| Start Weight | Weight Now | + /- |
|---|---|---|
| | | |

# 365 DAY WALKING CHALLENGE - WEEK 10

| Day/Date | Brief Route Info | | Walk No. 064 |
|---|---|---|---|
| | | | |

| Time Start | Time Walking | Distance | Avg Pace/Mile |
|---|---|---|---|
| | | | |

| Aches , Pains & Notes |
|---|
| |

| Day/Date | Brief Route Info | | Walk No. 065 |
|---|---|---|---|
| | | | |

| Time Start | Time Walking | Distance | Avg Pace/Mile |
|---|---|---|---|
| | | | |

| Aches , Pains & Notes |
|---|
| |

| Day/Date | Brief Route Info | | Walk No. 066 |
|---|---|---|---|
| | | | |

| Time Start | Time Walking | Distance | Avg Pace/Mile |
|---|---|---|---|
| | | | |

| Aches , Pains & Notes |
|---|
| |

| Day/Date | Brief Route Info | | Walk No. 067 |
|---|---|---|---|
| | | | |

| Time Start | Time Walking | Distance | Avg Pace/Mile |
|---|---|---|---|
| | | | |

| Aches , Pains & Notes |
|---|
| |

| Day/Date | Brief Route Info | | Walk No. 068 |
|---|---|---|---|
| | | | |

| Time Start | Time Walking | Distance | Avg Pace/Mile |
|---|---|---|---|
| | | | |

**Aches , Pains & Notes**

| |
|---|
| |

| Day/Date | Brief Route Info | | Walk No. 069 |
|---|---|---|---|
| | | | |

| Time Start | Time Walking | Distance | Avg Pace/Mile |
|---|---|---|---|
| | | | |

**Aches , Pains & Notes**

| |
|---|
| |

| Day/Date | Brief Route Info | | Walk No. 070 |
|---|---|---|---|
| | | | |

| Time Start | Time Walking | Distance | Avg Pace/Mile |
|---|---|---|---|
| | | | |

**Aches , Pains & Notes**

| |
|---|
| |

# SUMMARY

| Time Walking | Distance Walked | Average Pace |
|---|---|---|
| | | |

| Start Weight | Weight Now | + /- |
|---|---|---|
| | | |

# 365 DAY WALKING CHALLENGE - WEEK 11

| Day/Date | Brief Route Info | | Walk No. 071 |
|---|---|---|---|
| | | | |
| Time Start | Time Walking | Distance | Avg Pace/Mile |
| | | | |

**Aches , Pains & Notes**

| Day/Date | Brief Route Info | | Walk No. 072 |
|---|---|---|---|
| | | | |
| Time Start | Time Walking | Distance | Avg Pace/Mile |
| | | | |

**Aches , Pains & Notes**

| Day/Date | Brief Route Info | | Walk No. 073 |
|---|---|---|---|
| | | | |
| Time Start | Time Walking | Distance | Avg Pace/Mile |
| | | | |

**Aches , Pains & Notes**

| Day/Date | Brief Route Info | | Walk No. 074 |
|---|---|---|---|
| | | | |
| Time Start | Time Walking | Distance | Avg Pace/Mile |
| | | | |

**Aches , Pains & Notes**

| Day/Date | Brief Route Info | | Walk No. 075 |
|---|---|---|---|
| | | | |

| Time Start | Time Walking | Distance | Avg Pace/Mile |
|---|---|---|---|
| | | | |

**Aches , Pains & Notes**

| | | | |
|---|---|---|---|
| | | | |

| Day/Date | Brief Route Info | | Walk No. 076 |
|---|---|---|---|
| | | | |

| Time Start | Time Walking | Distance | Avg Pace/Mile |
|---|---|---|---|
| | | | |

**Aches , Pains & Notes**

| | | | |
|---|---|---|---|
| | | | |

| Day/Date | Brief Route Info | | Walk No. 077 |
|---|---|---|---|
| | | | |

| Time Start | Time Walking | Distance | Avg Pace/Mile |
|---|---|---|---|
| | | | |

**Aches , Pains & Notes**

| | | | |
|---|---|---|---|
| | | | |

# SUMMARY

| Time Walking | Distance Walked | Average Pace |
|---|---|---|
| | | |

| Start Weight | Weight Now | + /- |
|---|---|---|
| | | |

# 365 DAY WALKING CHALLENGE - WEEK 12

| Day/Date | Brief Route Info | | Walk No. 078 |
|---|---|---|---|
| | | | |

| Time Start | Time Walking | Distance | Avg Pace/Mile |
|---|---|---|---|
| | | | |

| Aches , Pains & Notes | | | |
|---|---|---|---|
| | | | |

| Day/Date | Brief Route Info | | Walk No. 079 |
|---|---|---|---|
| | | | |

| Time Start | Time Walking | Distance | Avg Pace/Mile |
|---|---|---|---|
| | | | |

| Aches , Pains & Notes | | | |
|---|---|---|---|
| | | | |

| Day/Date | Brief Route Info | | Walk No. 080 |
|---|---|---|---|
| | | | |

| Time Start | Time Walking | Distance | Avg Pace/Mile |
|---|---|---|---|
| | | | |

| Aches , Pains & Notes | | | |
|---|---|---|---|
| | | | |

| Day/Date | Brief Route Info | | Walk No. 081 |
|---|---|---|---|
| | | | |

| Time Start | Time Walking | Distance | Avg Pace/Mile |
|---|---|---|---|
| | | | |

| Aches , Pains & Notes | | | |
|---|---|---|---|
| | | | |

| Day/Date | Brief Route Info | | Walk No. 082 |
|---|---|---|---|
| | | | |

| Time Start | Time Walking | Distance | Avg Pace/Mile |
|---|---|---|---|
| | | | |

**Aches , Pains & Notes**

| |
|---|
| |

| Day/Date | Brief Route Info | | Walk No. 083 |
|---|---|---|---|
| | | | |

| Time Start | Time Walking | Distance | Avg Pace/Mile |
|---|---|---|---|
| | | | |

**Aches , Pains & Notes**

| |
|---|
| |

| Day/Date | Brief Route Info | | Walk No. 084 |
|---|---|---|---|
| | | | |

| Time Start | Time Walking | Distance | Avg Pace/Mile |
|---|---|---|---|
| | | | |

**Aches , Pains & Notes**

| |
|---|
| |

# SUMMARY

| Time Walking | Distance Walked | Average Pace |
|---|---|---|
| | | |

| Start Weight | Weight Now | + /- |
|---|---|---|
| | | |

# 365 DAY WALKING CHALLENGE - WEEK 13

| Day/Date | Brief Route Info | | Walk No. 085 |
|---|---|---|---|
| | | | |
| Time Start | Time Walking | Distance | Avg Pace/Mile |
| | | | |

**Aches , Pains & Notes**

| Day/Date | Brief Route Info | | Walk No. 086 |
|---|---|---|---|
| | | | |
| Time Start | Time Walking | Distance | Avg Pace/Mile |
| | | | |

**Aches , Pains & Notes**

| Day/Date | Brief Route Info | | Walk No. 087 |
|---|---|---|---|
| | | | |
| Time Start | Time Walking | Distance | Avg Pace/Mile |
| | | | |

**Aches , Pains & Notes**

| Day/Date | Brief Route Info | | Walk No. 088 |
|---|---|---|---|
| | | | |
| Time Start | Time Walking | Distance | Avg Pace/Mile |
| | | | |

**Aches , Pains & Notes**

| Day/Date | Brief Route Info | | Walk No. 089 |
|---|---|---|---|
| | | | |

| Time Start | Time Walking | Distance | Avg Pace/Mile |
|---|---|---|---|
| | | | |

**Aches , Pains & Notes**

| | | | |
|---|---|---|---|
| | | | |

| Day/Date | Brief Route Info | | Walk No. 090 |
|---|---|---|---|
| | | | |

| Time Start | Time Walking | Distance | Avg Pace/Mile |
|---|---|---|---|
| | | | |

**Aches , Pains & Notes**

| | | | |
|---|---|---|---|
| | | | |

| Day/Date | Brief Route Info | | Walk No. 091 |
|---|---|---|---|
| | | | |

| Time Start | Time Walking | Distance | Avg Pace/Mile |
|---|---|---|---|
| | | | |

**Aches , Pains & Notes**

| | | | |
|---|---|---|---|
| | | | |

# SUMMARY

| Time Walking | Distance Walked | Average Pace |
|---|---|---|
| | | |

| Start Weight | Weight Now | + /- |
|---|---|---|
| | | |

# 365 DAY WALKING CHALLENGE - WEEK 14

| Day/Date | Brief Route Info | | Walk No. 092 |
|---|---|---|---|
| | | | |
| Time Start | Time Walking | Distance | Avg Pace/Mile |
| | | | |
| Aches , Pains & Notes | | | |
| | | | |

| Day/Date | Brief Route Info | | Walk No. 093 |
|---|---|---|---|
| | | | |
| Time Start | Time Walking | Distance | Avg Pace/Mile |
| | | | |
| Aches , Pains & Notes | | | |
| | | | |

| Day/Date | Brief Route Info | | Walk No. 094 |
|---|---|---|---|
| | | | |
| Time Start | Time Walking | Distance | Avg Pace/Mile |
| | | | |
| Aches , Pains & Notes | | | |
| | | | |

| Day/Date | Brief Route Info | | Walk No. 095 |
|---|---|---|---|
| | | | |
| Time Start | Time Walking | Distance | Avg Pace/Mile |
| | | | |
| Aches , Pains & Notes | | | |
| | | | |

| Day/Date | Brief Route Info | | Walk No. 096 |
|---|---|---|---|
| | | | |

| Time Start | Time Walking | Distance | Avg Pace/Mile |
|---|---|---|---|
| | | | |

| Aches , Pains & Notes |
|---|
| |

| Day/Date | Brief Route Info | | Walk No. 097 |
|---|---|---|---|
| | | | |

| Time Start | Time Walking | Distance | Avg Pace/Mile |
|---|---|---|---|
| | | | |

| Aches , Pains & Notes |
|---|
| |

| Day/Date | Brief Route Info | | Walk No. 098 |
|---|---|---|---|
| | | | |

| Time Start | Time Walking | Distance | Avg Pace/Mile |
|---|---|---|---|
| | | | |

| Aches , Pains & Notes |
|---|
| |

# SUMMARY

| Time Walking | Distance Walked | Average Pace |
|---|---|---|
| | | |

| Start Weight | Weight Now | + /- |
|---|---|---|
| | | |

# 365 DAY WALKING CHALLENGE - WEEK 15

| Day/Date | Brief Route Info | | Walk No. 099 |
|---|---|---|---|
| | | | |

| Time Start | Time Walking | Distance | Avg Pace/Mile |
|---|---|---|---|
| | | | |

**Aches , Pains & Notes**

| | |
|---|---|
| | |

| Day/Date | Brief Route Info | | Walk No. 100 |
|---|---|---|---|
| | | | |

| Time Start | Time Walking | Distance | Avg Pace/Mile |
|---|---|---|---|
| | | | |

**Aches , Pains & Notes**

| | |
|---|---|
| | |

| Day/Date | Brief Route Info | | Walk No. 101 |
|---|---|---|---|
| | | | |

| Time Start | Time Walking | Distance | Avg Pace/Mile |
|---|---|---|---|
| | | | |

**Aches , Pains & Notes**

| | |
|---|---|
| | |

| Day/Date | Brief Route Info | | Walk No. 102 |
|---|---|---|---|
| | | | |

| Time Start | Time Walking | Distance | Avg Pace/Mile |
|---|---|---|---|
| | | | |

**Aches , Pains & Notes**

| | |
|---|---|
| | |

| Day/Date | Brief Route Info | | Walk No. 103 |
|---|---|---|---|
| | | | |

| Time Start | Time Walking | Distance | Avg Pace/Mile |
|---|---|---|---|
| | | | |

**Aches , Pains & Notes**

| |
|---|
| |

| Day/Date | Brief Route Info | | Walk No. 104 |
|---|---|---|---|
| | | | |

| Time Start | Time Walking | Distance | Avg Pace/Mile |
|---|---|---|---|
| | | | |

**Aches , Pains & Notes**

| |
|---|
| |

| Day/Date | Brief Route Info | | Walk No. 105 |
|---|---|---|---|
| | | | |

| Time Start | Time Walking | Distance | Avg Pace/Mile |
|---|---|---|---|
| | | | |

**Aches , Pains & Notes**

| |
|---|
| |

# SUMMARY

| Time Walking | Distance Walked | Average Pace |
|---|---|---|
| | | |

| Start Weight | Weight Now | + /- |
|---|---|---|
| | | |

# 365 DAY WALKING CHALLENGE - WEEK 16

| Day/Date | Brief Route Info | | Walk No. 106 |
|---|---|---|---|
| Time Start | Time Walking | Distance | Avg Pace/Mile |
| | | | |
| Aches , Pains & Notes | | | |
| | | | |

| Day/Date | Brief Route Info | | Walk No. 107 |
|---|---|---|---|
| Time Start | Time Walking | Distance | Avg Pace/Mile |
| | | | |
| Aches , Pains & Notes | | | |
| | | | |

| Day/Date | Brief Route Info | | Walk No. 108 |
|---|---|---|---|
| Time Start | Time Walking | Distance | Avg Pace/Mile |
| | | | |
| Aches , Pains & Notes | | | |
| | | | |

| Day/Date | Brief Route Info | | Walk No. 109 |
|---|---|---|---|
| Time Start | Time Walking | Distance | Avg Pace/Mile |
| | | | |
| Aches , Pains & Notes | | | |
| | | | |

| Day/Date | Brief Route Info | | Walk No. 110 |
|---|---|---|---|
| | | | |

| Time Start | Time Walking | Distance | Avg Pace/Mile |
|---|---|---|---|
| | | | |

**Aches , Pains & Notes**

| | | | |
|---|---|---|---|
| | | | |

| Day/Date | Brief Route Info | | Walk No. 111 |
|---|---|---|---|
| | | | |

| Time Start | Time Walking | Distance | Avg Pace/Mile |
|---|---|---|---|
| | | | |

**Aches , Pains & Notes**

| | | | |
|---|---|---|---|
| | | | |

| Day/Date | Brief Route Info | | Walk No. 112 |
|---|---|---|---|
| | | | |

| Time Start | Time Walking | Distance | Avg Pace/Mile |
|---|---|---|---|
| | | | |

**Aches , Pains & Notes**

| | | | |
|---|---|---|---|
| | | | |

# SUMMARY

| Time Walking | Distance Walked | Average Pace |
|---|---|---|
| | | |

| Start Weight | Weight Now | + /- |
|---|---|---|
| | | |

# 365 DAY WALKING CHALLENGE - WEEK 17

| Day/Date | Brief Route Info | | Walk No. 113 |
|---|---|---|---|
| | | | |
| Time Start | Time Walking | Distance | Avg Pace/Mile |
| | | | |

**Aches , Pains & Notes**

| | | | |
|---|---|---|---|
| | | | |

| Day/Date | Brief Route Info | | Walk No. 114 |
|---|---|---|---|
| | | | |
| Time Start | Time Walking | Distance | Avg Pace/Mile |
| | | | |

**Aches , Pains & Notes**

| | | | |
|---|---|---|---|
| | | | |

| Day/Date | Brief Route Info | | Walk No. 115 |
|---|---|---|---|
| | | | |
| Time Start | Time Walking | Distance | Avg Pace/Mile |
| | | | |

**Aches , Pains & Notes**

| | | | |
|---|---|---|---|
| | | | |

| Day/Date | Brief Route Info | | Walk No. 116 |
|---|---|---|---|
| | | | |
| Time Start | Time Walking | Distance | Avg Pace/Mile |
| | | | |

**Aches , Pains & Notes**

| | | | |
|---|---|---|---|
| | | | |

| Day/Date | Brief Route Info | | Walk No. 117 |
|---|---|---|---|
| | | | |

| Time Start | Time Walking | Distance | Avg Pace/Mile |
|---|---|---|---|
| | | | |

**Aches , Pains & Notes**

| |
|---|
| |

| Day/Date | Brief Route Info | | Walk No. 118 |
|---|---|---|---|
| | | | |

| Time Start | Time Walking | Distance | Avg Pace/Mile |
|---|---|---|---|
| | | | |

**Aches , Pains & Notes**

| |
|---|
| |

| Day/Date | Brief Route Info | | Walk No. 119 |
|---|---|---|---|
| | | | |

| Time Start | Time Walking | Distance | Avg Pace/Mile |
|---|---|---|---|
| | | | |

**Aches , Pains & Notes**

| |
|---|
| |

# SUMMARY

| Time Walking | Distance Walked | Average Pace |
|---|---|---|
| | | |

| Start Weight | Weight Now | + /- |
|---|---|---|
| | | |

# 365 DAY WALKING CHALLENGE - WEEK 18

| Day/Date | Brief Route Info | | Walk No. 120 |
|---|---|---|---|
| | | | |

| Time Start | Time Walking | Distance | Avg Pace/Mile |
|---|---|---|---|
| | | | |

**Aches , Pains & Notes**

| Day/Date | Brief Route Info | | Walk No. 121 |
|---|---|---|---|
| | | | |

| Time Start | Time Walking | Distance | Avg Pace/Mile |
|---|---|---|---|
| | | | |

**Aches , Pains & Notes**

| Day/Date | Brief Route Info | | Walk No. 122 |
|---|---|---|---|
| | | | |

| Time Start | Time Walking | Distance | Avg Pace/Mile |
|---|---|---|---|
| | | | |

**Aches , Pains & Notes**

| Day/Date | Brief Route Info | | Walk No. 123 |
|---|---|---|---|
| | | | |

| Time Start | Time Walking | Distance | Avg Pace/Mile |
|---|---|---|---|
| | | | |

**Aches , Pains & Notes**

| Day/Date | Brief Route Info | | Walk No. 124 |
|---|---|---|---|

| Time Start | Time Walking | Distance | Avg Pace/Mile |
|---|---|---|---|
| | | | |

**Aches , Pains & Notes**

| Day/Date | Brief Route Info | | Walk No. 125 |
|---|---|---|---|

| Time Start | Time Walking | Distance | Avg Pace/Mile |
|---|---|---|---|
| | | | |

**Aches , Pains & Notes**

| Day/Date | Brief Route Info | | Walk No. 126 |
|---|---|---|---|

| Time Start | Time Walking | Distance | Avg Pace/Mile |
|---|---|---|---|
| | | | |

**Aches , Pains & Notes**

# SUMMARY

| Time Walking | Distance Walked | Average Pace |
|---|---|---|
| | | |

| Start Weight | Weight Now | + /- |
|---|---|---|
| | | |

# 365 DAY WALKING CHALLENGE - WEEK 19

| Day/Date | Brief Route Info | | Walk No. 127 |
|---|---|---|---|
| | | | |
| Time Start | Time Walking | Distance | Avg Pace/Mile |
| | | | |
| Aches , Pains & Notes | | | |
| | | | |

| Day/Date | Brief Route Info | | Walk No. 128 |
|---|---|---|---|
| | | | |
| Time Start | Time Walking | Distance | Avg Pace/Mile |
| | | | |
| Aches , Pains & Notes | | | |
| | | | |

| Day/Date | Brief Route Info | | Walk No. 129 |
|---|---|---|---|
| | | | |
| Time Start | Time Walking | Distance | Avg Pace/Mile |
| | | | |
| Aches , Pains & Notes | | | |
| | | | |

| Day/Date | Brief Route Info | | Walk No. 130 |
|---|---|---|---|
| | | | |
| Time Start | Time Walking | Distance | Avg Pace/Mile |
| | | | |
| Aches , Pains & Notes | | | |
| | | | |

| Day/Date | Brief Route Info | | Walk No. 131 |
|---|---|---|---|
| | | | |

| Time Start | Time Walking | Distance | Avg Pace/Mile |
|---|---|---|---|
| | | | |

| Aches , Pains & Notes |
|---|
| |

| Day/Date | Brief Route Info | | Walk No. 132 |
|---|---|---|---|
| | | | |

| Time Start | Time Walking | Distance | Avg Pace/Mile |
|---|---|---|---|
| | | | |

| Aches , Pains & Notes |
|---|
| |

| Day/Date | Brief Route Info | | Walk No. 133 |
|---|---|---|---|
| | | | |

| Time Start | Time Walking | Distance | Avg Pace/Mile |
|---|---|---|---|
| | | | |

| Aches , Pains & Notes |
|---|
| |

# SUMMARY

| Time Walking | Distance Walked | Average Pace |
|---|---|---|
| | | |

| Start Weight | Weight Now | + /- |
|---|---|---|
| | | |

# 365 DAY WALKING CHALLENGE - WEEK 20

| Day/Date | Brief Route Info | | Walk No. 134 |
|---|---|---|---|
| Time Start | Time Walking | Distance | Avg Pace/Mile |
| | | | |

**Aches , Pains & Notes**

| Day/Date | Brief Route Info | | Walk No. 135 |
|---|---|---|---|
| Time Start | Time Walking | Distance | Avg Pace/Mile |
| | | | |

**Aches , Pains & Notes**

| Day/Date | Brief Route Info | | Walk No. 136 |
|---|---|---|---|
| Time Start | Time Walking | Distance | Avg Pace/Mile |
| | | | |

**Aches , Pains & Notes**

| Day/Date | Brief Route Info | | Walk No. 137 |
|---|---|---|---|
| Time Start | Time Walking | Distance | Avg Pace/Mile |
| | | | |

**Aches , Pains & Notes**

| Day/Date | Brief Route Info | | Walk No. 138 |
|---|---|---|---|

| Time Start | Time Walking | Distance | Avg Pace/Mile |
|---|---|---|---|
| | | | |

**Aches , Pains & Notes**

| Day/Date | Brief Route Info | | Walk No. 139 |
|---|---|---|---|

| Time Start | Time Walking | Distance | Avg Pace/Mile |
|---|---|---|---|
| | | | |

**Aches , Pains & Notes**

| Day/Date | Brief Route Info | | Walk No. 140 |
|---|---|---|---|

| Time Start | Time Walking | Distance | Avg Pace/Mile |
|---|---|---|---|
| | | | |

**Aches , Pains & Notes**

# SUMMARY

| Time Walking | Distance Walked | Average Pace |
|---|---|---|
| | | |

| Start Weight | Weight Now | + /- |
|---|---|---|
| | | |

# 365 DAY WALKING CHALLENGE - WEEK 21

| Day/Date | Brief Route Info | | Walk No. 141 |
|---|---|---|---|
| Time Start | Time Walking | Distance | Avg Pace/Mile |
| | | | |

**Aches , Pains & Notes**

| Day/Date | Brief Route Info | | Walk No. 142 |
|---|---|---|---|
| Time Start | Time Walking | Distance | Avg Pace/Mile |
| | | | |

**Aches , Pains & Notes**

| Day/Date | Brief Route Info | | Walk No. 143 |
|---|---|---|---|
| Time Start | Time Walking | Distance | Avg Pace/Mile |
| | | | |

**Aches , Pains & Notes**

| Day/Date | Brief Route Info | | Walk No. 144 |
|---|---|---|---|
| Time Start | Time Walking | Distance | Avg Pace/Mile |
| | | | |

**Aches , Pains & Notes**

| Day/Date | Brief Route Info | | Walk No. 145 |
|---|---|---|---|

| Time Start | Time Walking | Distance | Avg Pace/Mile |
|---|---|---|---|
| | | | |

**Aches , Pains & Notes**

| Day/Date | Brief Route Info | | Walk No. 146 |
|---|---|---|---|

| Time Start | Time Walking | Distance | Avg Pace/Mile |
|---|---|---|---|
| | | | |

**Aches , Pains & Notes**

| Day/Date | Brief Route Info | | Walk No. 147 |
|---|---|---|---|

| Time Start | Time Walking | Distance | Avg Pace/Mile |
|---|---|---|---|
| | | | |

**Aches , Pains & Notes**

# SUMMARY

| Time Walking | Distance Walked | Average Pace |
|---|---|---|
| | | |

| Start Weight | Weight Now | + /- |
|---|---|---|
| | | |

# 365 DAY WALKING CHALLENGE - WEEK 22

| Day/Date | Brief Route Info | | Walk No. 148 |
|---|---|---|---|
| | | | |

| Time Start | Time Walking | Distance | Avg Pace/Mile |
|---|---|---|---|
| | | | |

**Aches , Pains & Notes**

| | | | |
|---|---|---|---|
| | | | |

| Day/Date | Brief Route Info | | Walk No. 149 |
|---|---|---|---|
| | | | |

| Time Start | Time Walking | Distance | Avg Pace/Mile |
|---|---|---|---|
| | | | |

**Aches , Pains & Notes**

| | | | |
|---|---|---|---|
| | | | |

| Day/Date | Brief Route Info | | Walk No. 150 |
|---|---|---|---|
| | | | |

| Time Start | Time Walking | Distance | Avg Pace/Mile |
|---|---|---|---|
| | | | |

**Aches , Pains & Notes**

| | | | |
|---|---|---|---|
| | | | |

| Day/Date | Brief Route Info | | Walk No. 151 |
|---|---|---|---|
| | | | |

| Time Start | Time Walking | Distance | Avg Pace/Mile |
|---|---|---|---|
| | | | |

**Aches , Pains & Notes**

| | | | |
|---|---|---|---|
| | | | |

| Day/Date | Brief Route Info | | Walk No. 152 |
|---|---|---|---|

| Time Start | Time Walking | Distance | Avg Pace/Mile |
|---|---|---|---|
| | | | |

**Aches , Pains & Notes**

| Day/Date | Brief Route Info | | Walk No. 153 |
|---|---|---|---|

| Time Start | Time Walking | Distance | Avg Pace/Mile |
|---|---|---|---|
| | | | |

**Aches , Pains & Notes**

| Day/Date | Brief Route Info | | Walk No. 154 |
|---|---|---|---|

| Time Start | Time Walking | Distance | Avg Pace/Mile |
|---|---|---|---|
| | | | |

**Aches , Pains & Notes**

# SUMMARY

| Time Walking | Distance Walked | Average Pace |
|---|---|---|
| | | |

| Start Weight | Weight Now | + /- |
|---|---|---|
| | | |

# 365 DAY WALKING CHALLENGE - WEEK 23

| Day/Date | Brief Route Info | | Walk No. 155 |
|---|---|---|---|
| Time Start | Time Walking | Distance | Avg Pace/Mile |
| | | | |

**Aches , Pains & Notes**

| Day/Date | Brief Route Info | | Walk No. 156 |
|---|---|---|---|
| Time Start | Time Walking | Distance | Avg Pace/Mile |
| | | | |

**Aches , Pains & Notes**

| Day/Date | Brief Route Info | | Walk No. 157 |
|---|---|---|---|
| Time Start | Time Walking | Distance | Avg Pace/Mile |
| | | | |

**Aches , Pains & Notes**

| Day/Date | Brief Route Info | | Walk No. 158 |
|---|---|---|---|
| Time Start | Time Walking | Distance | Avg Pace/Mile |
| | | | |

**Aches , Pains & Notes**

| Day/Date | Brief Route Info | | Walk No. 159 |
|---|---|---|---|

| Time Start | Time Walking | Distance | Avg Pace/Mile |
|---|---|---|---|
| | | | |

**Aches , Pains & Notes**

| Day/Date | Brief Route Info | | Walk No. 160 |
|---|---|---|---|

| Time Start | Time Walking | Distance | Avg Pace/Mile |
|---|---|---|---|
| | | | |

**Aches , Pains & Notes**

| Day/Date | Brief Route Info | | Walk No. 161 |
|---|---|---|---|

| Time Start | Time Walking | Distance | Avg Pace/Mile |
|---|---|---|---|
| | | | |

**Aches , Pains & Notes**

# SUMMARY

| Time Walking | Distance Walked | Average Pace |
|---|---|---|
| | | |

| Start Weight | Weight Now | + /- |
|---|---|---|
| | | |

# 365 DAY WALKING CHALLENGE - WEEK 24

| Day/Date | Brief Route Info | | Walk No. 162 |
|---|---|---|---|
| Time Start | Time Walking | Distance | Avg Pace/Mile |
| | | | |

**Aches , Pains & Notes**

| Day/Date | Brief Route Info | | Walk No. 163 |
|---|---|---|---|
| Time Start | Time Walking | Distance | Avg Pace/Mile |
| | | | |

**Aches , Pains & Notes**

| Day/Date | Brief Route Info | | Walk No. 164 |
|---|---|---|---|
| Time Start | Time Walking | Distance | Avg Pace/Mile |
| | | | |

**Aches , Pains & Notes**

| Day/Date | Brief Route Info | | Walk No. 165 |
|---|---|---|---|
| Time Start | Time Walking | Distance | Avg Pace/Mile |
| | | | |

**Aches , Pains & Notes**

| Day/Date | Brief Route Info | | Walk No. 166 |
|---|---|---|---|
| | | | |

| Time Start | Time Walking | Distance | Avg Pace/Mile |
|---|---|---|---|
| | | | |

**Aches , Pains & Notes**

| | | | |
|---|---|---|---|
| | | | |

| Day/Date | Brief Route Info | | Walk No. 167 |
|---|---|---|---|
| | | | |

| Time Start | Time Walking | Distance | Avg Pace/Mile |
|---|---|---|---|
| | | | |

**Aches , Pains & Notes**

| | | | |
|---|---|---|---|
| | | | |

| Day/Date | Brief Route Info | | Walk No. 168 |
|---|---|---|---|
| | | | |

| Time Start | Time Walking | Distance | Avg Pace/Mile |
|---|---|---|---|
| | | | |

**Aches , Pains & Notes**

| | | | |
|---|---|---|---|
| | | | |

# SUMMARY

| Time Walking | Distance Walked | Average Pace |
|---|---|---|
| | | |

| Start Weight | Weight Now | + /- |
|---|---|---|
| | | |

# 365 DAY WALKING CHALLENGE - WEEK 25

| Day/Date | Brief Route Info | | Walk No. 169 |
|---|---|---|---|
| | | | |
| Time Start | Time Walking | Distance | Avg Pace/Mile |
| | | | |

**Aches , Pains & Notes**

| Day/Date | Brief Route Info | | Walk No. 170 |
|---|---|---|---|
| | | | |
| Time Start | Time Walking | Distance | Avg Pace/Mile |
| | | | |

**Aches , Pains & Notes**

| Day/Date | Brief Route Info | | Walk No. 171 |
|---|---|---|---|
| | | | |
| Time Start | Time Walking | Distance | Avg Pace/Mile |
| | | | |

**Aches , Pains & Notes**

| Day/Date | Brief Route Info | | Walk No. 172 |
|---|---|---|---|
| | | | |
| Time Start | Time Walking | Distance | Avg Pace/Mile |
| | | | |

**Aches , Pains & Notes**

| Day/Date | Brief Route Info | | Walk No. 173 |
|---|---|---|---|
| | | | |

| Time Start | Time Walking | Distance | Avg Pace/Mile |
|---|---|---|---|
| | | | |

**Aches , Pains & Notes**

| Day/Date | Brief Route Info | | Walk No. 174 |
|---|---|---|---|
| | | | |

| Time Start | Time Walking | Distance | Avg Pace/Mile |
|---|---|---|---|
| | | | |

**Aches , Pains & Notes**

| Day/Date | Brief Route Info | | Walk No. 175 |
|---|---|---|---|
| | | | |

| Time Start | Time Walking | Distance | Avg Pace/Mile |
|---|---|---|---|
| | | | |

**Aches , Pains & Notes**

# SUMMARY

| Time Walking | Distance Walked | Average Pace |
|---|---|---|
| | | |

| Start Weight | Weight Now | + /- |
|---|---|---|
| | | |

# 365 DAY WALKING CHALLENGE - WEEK 26

| Day/Date | Brief Route Info | | Walk No. 176 |
|---|---|---|---|
| Time Start | Time Walking | Distance | Avg Pace/Mile |
| | | | |

**Aches , Pains & Notes**

| Day/Date | Brief Route Info | | Walk No. 177 |
|---|---|---|---|
| Time Start | Time Walking | Distance | Avg Pace/Mile |
| | | | |

**Aches , Pains & Notes**

| Day/Date | Brief Route Info | | Walk No. 178 |
|---|---|---|---|
| Time Start | Time Walking | Distance | Avg Pace/Mile |
| | | | |

**Aches , Pains & Notes**

| Day/Date | Brief Route Info | | Walk No. 179 |
|---|---|---|---|
| Time Start | Time Walking | Distance | Avg Pace/Mile |
| | | | |

**Aches , Pains & Notes**

| Day/Date | Brief Route Info | | Walk No. 180 |
|---|---|---|---|
| | | | |

| Time Start | Time Walking | Distance | Avg Pace/Mile |
|---|---|---|---|
| | | | |

| Aches , Pains & Notes |
|---|
| |

| Day/Date | Brief Route Info | | Walk No. 181 |
|---|---|---|---|
| | | | |

| Time Start | Time Walking | Distance | Avg Pace/Mile |
|---|---|---|---|
| | | | |

| Aches , Pains & Notes |
|---|
| |

| Day/Date | Brief Route Info | | Walk No. 182 |
|---|---|---|---|
| | | | |

| Time Start | Time Walking | Distance | Avg Pace/Mile |
|---|---|---|---|
| | | | |

| Aches , Pains & Notes |
|---|
| |

# SUMMARY

| Time Walking | Distance Walked | Average Pace |
|---|---|---|
| | | |

| Start Weight | Weight Now | + /- |
|---|---|---|
| | | |

# 365 DAY WALKING CHALLENGE - WEEK 27

| Day/Date | Brief Route Info | | Walk No. 183 |
|---|---|---|---|
| | | | |
| Time Start | Time Walking | Distance | Avg Pace/Mile |
| | | | |

**Aches , Pains & Notes**

| Day/Date | Brief Route Info | | Walk No. 184 |
|---|---|---|---|
| | | | |
| Time Start | Time Walking | Distance | Avg Pace/Mile |
| | | | |

**Aches , Pains & Notes**

| Day/Date | Brief Route Info | | Walk No. 185 |
|---|---|---|---|
| | | | |
| Time Start | Time Walking | Distance | Avg Pace/Mile |
| | | | |

**Aches , Pains & Notes**

| Day/Date | Brief Route Info | | Walk No. 186 |
|---|---|---|---|
| | | | |
| Time Start | Time Walking | Distance | Avg Pace/Mile |
| | | | |

**Aches , Pains & Notes**

| Day/Date | Brief Route Info | | Walk No. 187 |
|---|---|---|---|
| | | | |

| Time Start | Time Walking | Distance | Avg Pace/Mile |
|---|---|---|---|
| | | | |

**Aches , Pains & Notes**

| | | | |
|---|---|---|---|
| | | | |

| Day/Date | Brief Route Info | | Walk No. 188 |
|---|---|---|---|
| | | | |

| Time Start | Time Walking | Distance | Avg Pace/Mile |
|---|---|---|---|
| | | | |

**Aches , Pains & Notes**

| | | | |
|---|---|---|---|
| | | | |

| Day/Date | Brief Route Info | | Walk No. 189 |
|---|---|---|---|
| | | | |

| Time Start | Time Walking | Distance | Avg Pace/Mile |
|---|---|---|---|
| | | | |

**Aches , Pains & Notes**

| | | | |
|---|---|---|---|
| | | | |

# SUMMARY

| Time Walking | Distance Walked | Average Pace |
|---|---|---|
| | | |

| Start Weight | Weight Now | + /- |
|---|---|---|
| | | |

# 365 DAY WALKING CHALLENGE - WEEK 28

| Day/Date | Brief Route Info | | Walk No. 190 |
|---|---|---|---|
| | | | |
| Time Start | Time Walking | Distance | Avg Pace/Mile |
| | | | |

**Aches , Pains & Notes**

| Day/Date | Brief Route Info | | Walk No. 191 |
|---|---|---|---|
| | | | |
| Time Start | Time Walking | Distance | Avg Pace/Mile |
| | | | |

**Aches , Pains & Notes**

| Day/Date | Brief Route Info | | Walk No. 192 |
|---|---|---|---|
| | | | |
| Time Start | Time Walking | Distance | Avg Pace/Mile |
| | | | |

**Aches , Pains & Notes**

| Day/Date | Brief Route Info | | Walk No. 193 |
|---|---|---|---|
| | | | |
| Time Start | Time Walking | Distance | Avg Pace/Mile |
| | | | |

**Aches , Pains & Notes**

| Day/Date | Brief Route Info | | Walk No. 194 |
|---|---|---|---|

| Time Start | Time Walking | Distance | Avg Pace/Mile |
|---|---|---|---|
| | | | |

**Aches , Pains & Notes**

| Day/Date | Brief Route Info | | Walk No. 195 |
|---|---|---|---|

| Time Start | Time Walking | Distance | Avg Pace/Mile |
|---|---|---|---|
| | | | |

**Aches , Pains & Notes**

| Day/Date | Brief Route Info | | Walk No. 196 |
|---|---|---|---|

| Time Start | Time Walking | Distance | Avg Pace/Mile |
|---|---|---|---|
| | | | |

**Aches , Pains & Notes**

# SUMMARY

| Time Walking | Distance Walked | Average Pace |
|---|---|---|
| | | |

| Start Weight | Weight Now | + /- |
|---|---|---|
| | | |

# 365 DAY WALKING CHALLENGE - WEEK 29

| Day/Date | Brief Route Info | | Walk No. 197 |
|---|---|---|---|
| Time Start | Time Walking | Distance | Avg Pace/Mile |
| | | | |

| Aches , Pains & Notes |
|---|
| |

| Day/Date | Brief Route Info | | Walk No. 198 |
|---|---|---|---|
| Time Start | Time Walking | Distance | Avg Pace/Mile |
| | | | |

| Aches , Pains & Notes |
|---|
| |

| Day/Date | Brief Route Info | | Walk No. 199 |
|---|---|---|---|
| Time Start | Time Walking | Distance | Avg Pace/Mile |
| | | | |

| Aches , Pains & Notes |
|---|
| |

| Day/Date | Brief Route Info | | Walk No. 200 |
|---|---|---|---|
| Time Start | Time Walking | Distance | Avg Pace/Mile |
| | | | |

| Aches , Pains & Notes |
|---|
| |

| Day/Date | Brief Route Info | | Walk No. 201 |
|---|---|---|---|
| | | | |

| Time Start | Time Walking | Distance | Avg Pace/Mile |
|---|---|---|---|
| | | | |

**Aches , Pains & Notes**

| | | | |
|---|---|---|---|

| Day/Date | Brief Route Info | | Walk No. 202 |
|---|---|---|---|
| | | | |

| Time Start | Time Walking | Distance | Avg Pace/Mile |
|---|---|---|---|
| | | | |

**Aches , Pains & Notes**

| | | | |
|---|---|---|---|

| Day/Date | Brief Route Info | | Walk No. 203 |
|---|---|---|---|
| | | | |

| Time Start | Time Walking | Distance | Avg Pace/Mile |
|---|---|---|---|
| | | | |

**Aches , Pains & Notes**

| | | | |
|---|---|---|---|

# SUMMARY

| Time Walking | Distance Walked | Average Pace |
|---|---|---|
| | | |

| Start Weight | Weight Now | + /- |
|---|---|---|
| | | |

# 365 DAY WALKING CHALLENGE – WEEK 30

| Day/Date | Brief Route Info | | Walk No. 204 |
|---|---|---|---|
| | | | |

| Time Start | Time Walking | Distance | Avg Pace/Mile |
|---|---|---|---|
| | | | |

**Aches , Pains & Notes**

| Day/Date | Brief Route Info | | Walk No. 205 |
|---|---|---|---|
| | | | |

| Time Start | Time Walking | Distance | Avg Pace/Mile |
|---|---|---|---|
| | | | |

**Aches , Pains & Notes**

| Day/Date | Brief Route Info | | Walk No. 206 |
|---|---|---|---|
| | | | |

| Time Start | Time Walking | Distance | Avg Pace/Mile |
|---|---|---|---|
| | | | |

**Aches , Pains & Notes**

| Day/Date | Brief Route Info | | Walk No. 207 |
|---|---|---|---|
| | | | |

| Time Start | Time Walking | Distance | Avg Pace/Mile |
|---|---|---|---|
| | | | |

**Aches , Pains & Notes**

| Day/Date | Brief Route Info | | Walk No. 208 |
|---|---|---|---|
| | | | |

| Time Start | Time Walking | Distance | Avg Pace/Mile |
|---|---|---|---|
| | | | |

**Aches , Pains & Notes**

| |
|---|
| |

| Day/Date | Brief Route Info | | Walk No. 209 |
|---|---|---|---|
| | | | |

| Time Start | Time Walking | Distance | Avg Pace/Mile |
|---|---|---|---|
| | | | |

**Aches , Pains & Notes**

| |
|---|
| |

| Day/Date | Brief Route Info | | Walk No. 210 |
|---|---|---|---|
| | | | |

| Time Start | Time Walking | Distance | Avg Pace/Mile |
|---|---|---|---|
| | | | |

**Aches , Pains & Notes**

| |
|---|
| |

# SUMMARY

| Time Walking | Distance Walked | Average Pace |
|---|---|---|
| | | |

| Start Weight | Weight Now | + /- |
|---|---|---|
| | | |

# 365 DAY WALKING CHALLENGE - WEEK 31

| Day/Date | Brief Route Info | | Walk No. 211 |
|---|---|---|---|
| Time Start | Time Walking | Distance | Avg Pace/Mile |
| | | | |

**Aches , Pains & Notes**

| Day/Date | Brief Route Info | | Walk No. 212 |
|---|---|---|---|
| Time Start | Time Walking | Distance | Avg Pace/Mile |
| | | | |

**Aches , Pains & Notes**

| Day/Date | Brief Route Info | | Walk No. 213 |
|---|---|---|---|
| Time Start | Time Walking | Distance | Avg Pace/Mile |
| | | | |

**Aches , Pains & Notes**

| Day/Date | Brief Route Info | | Walk No. 214 |
|---|---|---|---|
| Time Start | Time Walking | Distance | Avg Pace/Mile |
| | | | |

**Aches , Pains & Notes**

| Day/Date | Brief Route Info | | Walk No. 215 |
|---|---|---|---|
| | | | |

| Time Start | Time Walking | Distance | Avg Pace/Mile |
|---|---|---|---|
| | | | |

**Aches , Pains & Notes**

| | |
|---|---|
| | |

| Day/Date | Brief Route Info | | Walk No. 216 |
|---|---|---|---|
| | | | |

| Time Start | Time Walking | Distance | Avg Pace/Mile |
|---|---|---|---|
| | | | |

**Aches , Pains & Notes**

| | |
|---|---|
| | |

| Day/Date | Brief Route Info | | Walk No. 217 |
|---|---|---|---|
| | | | |

| Time Start | Time Walking | Distance | Avg Pace/Mile |
|---|---|---|---|
| | | | |

**Aches , Pains & Notes**

| | |
|---|---|
| | |

# SUMMARY

| Time Walking | Distance Walked | Average Pace |
|---|---|---|
| | | |

| Start Weight | Weight Now | + /- |
|---|---|---|
| | | |

# 365 DAY WALKING CHALLENGE - WEEK 32

| Day/Date | Brief Route Info | | Walk No. 218 |
|---|---|---|---|
| **Time Start** | **Time Walking** | **Distance** | **Avg Pace/Mile** |
| | | | |

**Aches , Pains & Notes**



| Day/Date | Brief Route Info | | Walk No. 219 |
|---|---|---|---|
| **Time Start** | **Time Walking** | **Distance** | **Avg Pace/Mile** |
| | | | |

**Aches , Pains & Notes**



| Day/Date | Brief Route Info | | Walk No. 220 |
|---|---|---|---|
| **Time Start** | **Time Walking** | **Distance** | **Avg Pace/Mile** |
| | | | |

**Aches , Pains & Notes**



| Day/Date | Brief Route Info | | Walk No. 221 |
|---|---|---|---|
| **Time Start** | **Time Walking** | **Distance** | **Avg Pace/Mile** |
| | | | |

**Aches , Pains & Notes**

| Day/Date | Brief Route Info | | Walk No. 222 |
|---|---|---|---|
| | | | |

| Time Start | Time Walking | Distance | Avg Pace/Mile |
|---|---|---|---|
| | | | |

**Aches , Pains & Notes**

| Day/Date | Brief Route Info | | Walk No. 223 |
|---|---|---|---|
| | | | |

| Time Start | Time Walking | Distance | Avg Pace/Mile |
|---|---|---|---|
| | | | |

**Aches , Pains & Notes**

| Day/Date | Brief Route Info | | Walk No. 224 |
|---|---|---|---|
| | | | |

| Time Start | Time Walking | Distance | Avg Pace/Mile |
|---|---|---|---|
| | | | |

**Aches , Pains & Notes**

# SUMMARY

| Time Walking | Distance Walked | Average Pace |
|---|---|---|
| | | |

| Start Weight | Weight Now | + /- |
|---|---|---|
| | | |

# 365 DAY WALKING CHALLENGE - WEEK 33

| Day/Date | Brief Route Info | | Walk No. 225 |
|---|---|---|---|
| **Time Start** | **Time Walking** | **Distance** | **Avg Pace/Mile** |
| | | | |
| **Aches , Pains & Notes** | | | |
| | | | |

| Day/Date | Brief Route Info | | Walk No. 226 |
|---|---|---|---|
| **Time Start** | **Time Walking** | **Distance** | **Avg Pace/Mile** |
| | | | |
| **Aches , Pains & Notes** | | | |
| | | | |

| Day/Date | Brief Route Info | | Walk No. 227 |
|---|---|---|---|
| **Time Start** | **Time Walking** | **Distance** | **Avg Pace/Mile** |
| | | | |
| **Aches , Pains & Notes** | | | |
| | | | |

| Day/Date | Brief Route Info | | Walk No. 228 |
|---|---|---|---|
| **Time Start** | **Time Walking** | **Distance** | **Avg Pace/Mile** |
| | | | |
| **Aches , Pains & Notes** | | | |
| | | | |

| Day/Date | Brief Route Info | | Walk No. 229 |
|---|---|---|---|

| Time Start | Time Walking | Distance | Avg Pace/Mile |
|---|---|---|---|
| | | | |

**Aches , Pains & Notes**

| Day/Date | Brief Route Info | | Walk No. 230 |
|---|---|---|---|

| Time Start | Time Walking | Distance | Avg Pace/Mile |
|---|---|---|---|
| | | | |

**Aches , Pains & Notes**

| Day/Date | Brief Route Info | | Walk No. 231 |
|---|---|---|---|

| Time Start | Time Walking | Distance | Avg Pace/Mile |
|---|---|---|---|
| | | | |

**Aches , Pains & Notes**

# SUMMARY

| Time Walking | Distance Walked | Average Pace |
|---|---|---|
| | | |

| Start Weight | Weight Now | + /- |
|---|---|---|
| | | |

# 365 DAY WALKING CHALLENGE - WEEK 34

| Day/Date | Brief Route Info | | Walk No. 232 |
|---|---|---|---|
| | | | |
| Time Start | Time Walking | Distance | Avg Pace/Mile |
| | | | |

**Aches , Pains & Notes**

| Day/Date | Brief Route Info | | Walk No. 233 |
|---|---|---|---|
| | | | |
| Time Start | Time Walking | Distance | Avg Pace/Mile |
| | | | |

**Aches , Pains & Notes**

| Day/Date | Brief Route Info | | Walk No. 234 |
|---|---|---|---|
| | | | |
| Time Start | Time Walking | Distance | Avg Pace/Mile |
| | | | |

**Aches , Pains & Notes**

| Day/Date | Brief Route Info | | Walk No. 235 |
|---|---|---|---|
| | | | |
| Time Start | Time Walking | Distance | Avg Pace/Mile |
| | | | |

**Aches , Pains & Notes**

| Day/Date | Brief Route Info | | Walk No. 236 |
|---|---|---|---|
| | | | |

| Time Start | Time Walking | Distance | Avg Pace/Mile |
|---|---|---|---|
| | | | |

**Aches , Pains & Notes**

| Day/Date | Brief Route Info | | Walk No. 237 |
|---|---|---|---|
| | | | |

| Time Start | Time Walking | Distance | Avg Pace/Mile |
|---|---|---|---|
| | | | |

**Aches , Pains & Notes**

| Day/Date | Brief Route Info | | Walk No. 238 |
|---|---|---|---|
| | | | |

| Time Start | Time Walking | Distance | Avg Pace/Mile |
|---|---|---|---|
| | | | |

**Aches , Pains & Notes**

# SUMMARY

| Time Walking | Distance Walked | Average Pace |
|---|---|---|
| | | |

| Start Weight | Weight Now | + /- |
|---|---|---|
| | | |

# 365 DAY WALKING CHALLENGE - WEEK 35

| Day/Date | Brief Route Info | | Walk No. 239 |
|---|---|---|---|
| | | | |
| Time Start | Time Walking | Distance | Avg Pace/Mile |
| | | | |
| Aches , Pains & Notes | | | |
| | | | |

| Day/Date | Brief Route Info | | Walk No. 240 |
|---|---|---|---|
| | | | |
| Time Start | Time Walking | Distance | Avg Pace/Mile |
| | | | |
| Aches , Pains & Notes | | | |
| | | | |

| Day/Date | Brief Route Info | | Walk No. 241 |
|---|---|---|---|
| | | | |
| Time Start | Time Walking | Distance | Avg Pace/Mile |
| | | | |
| Aches , Pains & Notes | | | |
| | | | |

| Day/Date | Brief Route Info | | Walk No. 242 |
|---|---|---|---|
| | | | |
| Time Start | Time Walking | Distance | Avg Pace/Mile |
| | | | |
| Aches , Pains & Notes | | | |
| | | | |

| Day/Date | Brief Route Info | | Walk No. 243 |
|---|---|---|---|
| | | | |

| Time Start | Time Walking | Distance | Avg Pace/Mile |
|---|---|---|---|
| | | | |

**Aches , Pains & Notes**

| |
|---|
| |

| Day/Date | Brief Route Info | | Walk No. 244 |
|---|---|---|---|
| | | | |

| Time Start | Time Walking | Distance | Avg Pace/Mile |
|---|---|---|---|
| | | | |

**Aches , Pains & Notes**

| |
|---|
| |

| Day/Date | Brief Route Info | | Walk No. 245 |
|---|---|---|---|
| | | | |

| Time Start | Time Walking | Distance | Avg Pace/Mile |
|---|---|---|---|
| | | | |

**Aches , Pains & Notes**

| |
|---|
| |

# SUMMARY

| Time Walking | Distance Walked | Average Pace |
|---|---|---|
| | | |

| Start Weight | Weight Now | + /- |
|---|---|---|
| | | |

# 365 DAY WALKING CHALLENGE - WEEK 36

| Day/Date | Brief Route Info | | Walk No. 246 |
|---|---|---|---|
| | | | |

| Time Start | Time Walking | Distance | Avg Pace/Mile |
|---|---|---|---|
| | | | |

| Aches , Pains & Notes |
|---|
| |

| Day/Date | Brief Route Info | | Walk No. 247 |
|---|---|---|---|
| | | | |

| Time Start | Time Walking | Distance | Avg Pace/Mile |
|---|---|---|---|
| | | | |

| Aches , Pains & Notes |
|---|
| |

| Day/Date | Brief Route Info | | Walk No. 248 |
|---|---|---|---|
| | | | |

| Time Start | Time Walking | Distance | Avg Pace/Mile |
|---|---|---|---|
| | | | |

| Aches , Pains & Notes |
|---|
| |

| Day/Date | Brief Route Info | | Walk No. 249 |
|---|---|---|---|
| | | | |

| Time Start | Time Walking | Distance | Avg Pace/Mile |
|---|---|---|---|
| | | | |

| Aches , Pains & Notes |
|---|
| |

| Day/Date | Brief Route Info | | Walk No. 250 |
|---|---|---|---|
| | | | |

| Time Start | Time Walking | Distance | Avg Pace/Mile |
|---|---|---|---|
| | | | |

| Aches , Pains & Notes |
|---|
| |

| Day/Date | Brief Route Info | | Walk No. 251 |
|---|---|---|---|
| | | | |

| Time Start | Time Walking | Distance | Avg Pace/Mile |
|---|---|---|---|
| | | | |

| Aches , Pains & Notes |
|---|
| |

| Day/Date | Brief Route Info | | Walk No. 252 |
|---|---|---|---|
| | | | |

| Time Start | Time Walking | Distance | Avg Pace/Mile |
|---|---|---|---|
| | | | |

| Aches , Pains & Notes |
|---|
| |

# SUMMARY

| Time Walking | Distance Walked | Average Pace |
|---|---|---|
| | | |

| Start Weight | Weight Now | + /- |
|---|---|---|
| | | |

# 365 DAY WALKING CHALLENGE - WEEK 37

| Day/Date | Brief Route Info | | Walk No. 253 |
|---|---|---|---|
| | | | |
| Time Start | Time Walking | Distance | Avg Pace/Mile |
| | | | |

**Aches , Pains & Notes**

| Day/Date | Brief Route Info | | Walk No. 254 |
|---|---|---|---|
| | | | |
| Time Start | Time Walking | Distance | Avg Pace/Mile |
| | | | |

**Aches , Pains & Notes**

| Day/Date | Brief Route Info | | Walk No. 255 |
|---|---|---|---|
| | | | |
| Time Start | Time Walking | Distance | Avg Pace/Mile |
| | | | |

**Aches , Pains & Notes**

| Day/Date | Brief Route Info | | Walk No. 256 |
|---|---|---|---|
| | | | |
| Time Start | Time Walking | Distance | Avg Pace/Mile |
| | | | |

**Aches , Pains & Notes**

| Day/Date | Brief Route Info | | Walk No. 257 |
|---|---|---|---|
| | | | |

| Time Start | Time Walking | Distance | Avg Pace/Mile |
|---|---|---|---|
| | | | |

**Aches , Pains & Notes**

| | | | |
|---|---|---|---|
| | | | |

| Day/Date | Brief Route Info | | Walk No. 258 |
|---|---|---|---|
| | | | |

| Time Start | Time Walking | Distance | Avg Pace/Mile |
|---|---|---|---|
| | | | |

**Aches , Pains & Notes**

| | | | |
|---|---|---|---|
| | | | |

| Day/Date | Brief Route Info | | Walk No. 259 |
|---|---|---|---|
| | | | |

| Time Start | Time Walking | Distance | Avg Pace/Mile |
|---|---|---|---|
| | | | |

**Aches , Pains & Notes**

| | | | |
|---|---|---|---|
| | | | |

# SUMMARY

| Time Walking | Distance Walked | Average Pace |
|---|---|---|
| | | |

| Start Weight | Weight Now | + /- |
|---|---|---|
| | | |

# 365 DAY WALKING CHALLENGE - WEEK 38

| Day/Date | Brief Route Info | | Walk No. 260 |
|---|---|---|---|
| | | | |
| Time Start | Time Walking | Distance | Avg Pace/Mile |
| | | | |
| Aches , Pains & Notes | | | |
| | | | |

| Day/Date | Brief Route Info | | Walk No. 261 |
|---|---|---|---|
| | | | |
| Time Start | Time Walking | Distance | Avg Pace/Mile |
| | | | |
| Aches , Pains & Notes | | | |
| | | | |

| Day/Date | Brief Route Info | | Walk No. 262 |
|---|---|---|---|
| | | | |
| Time Start | Time Walking | Distance | Avg Pace/Mile |
| | | | |
| Aches , Pains & Notes | | | |
| | | | |

| Day/Date | Brief Route Info | | Walk No. 263 |
|---|---|---|---|
| | | | |
| Time Start | Time Walking | Distance | Avg Pace/Mile |
| | | | |
| Aches , Pains & Notes | | | |
| | | | |

| Day/Date | Brief Route Info | | Walk No. 264 |
|---|---|---|---|
| | | | |

| Time Start | Time Walking | Distance | Avg Pace/Mile |
|---|---|---|---|
| | | | |

**Aches , Pains & Notes**

| Day/Date | Brief Route Info | | Walk No. 265 |
|---|---|---|---|
| | | | |

| Time Start | Time Walking | Distance | Avg Pace/Mile |
|---|---|---|---|
| | | | |

**Aches , Pains & Notes**

| Day/Date | Brief Route Info | | Walk No. 266 |
|---|---|---|---|
| | | | |

| Time Start | Time Walking | Distance | Avg Pace/Mile |
|---|---|---|---|
| | | | |

**Aches , Pains & Notes**

# SUMMARY

| Time Walking | Distance Walked | Average Pace |
|---|---|---|
| | | |

| Start Weight | Weight Now | + /- |
|---|---|---|
| | | |

# 365 DAY WALKING CHALLENGE - WEEK 39

| Day/Date | Brief Route Info | Walk No. 267 |
|----------|------------------|--------------|
|          |                  |              |

| Time Start | Time Walking | Distance | Avg Pace/Mile |
|------------|--------------|----------|---------------|
|            |              |          |               |

**Aches , Pains & Notes**

| Day/Date | Brief Route Info | Walk No. 268 |
|----------|------------------|--------------|
|          |                  |              |

| Time Start | Time Walking | Distance | Avg Pace/Mile |
|------------|--------------|----------|---------------|
|            |              |          |               |

**Aches , Pains & Notes**

| Day/Date | Brief Route Info | Walk No. 269 |
|----------|------------------|--------------|
|          |                  |              |

| Time Start | Time Walking | Distance | Avg Pace/Mile |
|------------|--------------|----------|---------------|
|            |              |          |               |

**Aches , Pains & Notes**

| Day/Date | Brief Route Info | Walk No. 270 |
|----------|------------------|--------------|
|          |                  |              |

| Time Start | Time Walking | Distance | Avg Pace/Mile |
|------------|--------------|----------|---------------|
|            |              |          |               |

**Aches , Pains & Notes**

| Day/Date | Brief Route Info | Walk No. 271 |
|---|---|---|

| Time Start | Time Walking | Distance | Avg Pace/Mile |
|---|---|---|---|
| | | | |

**Aches , Pains & Notes**

| Day/Date | Brief Route Info | Walk No. 272 |
|---|---|---|

| Time Start | Time Walking | Distance | Avg Pace/Mile |
|---|---|---|---|
| | | | |

**Aches , Pains & Notes**

| Day/Date | Brief Route Info | Walk No. 273 |
|---|---|---|

| Time Start | Time Walking | Distance | Avg Pace/Mile |
|---|---|---|---|
| | | | |

**Aches , Pains & Notes**

# SUMMARY

| Time Walking | Distance Walked | Average Pace |
|---|---|---|
| | | |

| Start Weight | Weight Now | + /- |
|---|---|---|
| | | |

# 365 DAY WALKING CHALLENGE – WEEK 40

| Day/Date | Brief Route Info | | Walk No. 274 |
|---|---|---|---|
| Time Start | Time Walking | Distance | Avg Pace/Mile |
| | | | |

**Aches , Pains & Notes**

| Day/Date | Brief Route Info | | Walk No. 275 |
|---|---|---|---|
| Time Start | Time Walking | Distance | Avg Pace/Mile |
| | | | |

**Aches , Pains & Notes**

| Day/Date | Brief Route Info | | Walk No. 276 |
|---|---|---|---|
| Time Start | Time Walking | Distance | Avg Pace/Mile |
| | | | |

**Aches , Pains & Notes**

| Day/Date | Brief Route Info | | Walk No. 277 |
|---|---|---|---|
| Time Start | Time Walking | Distance | Avg Pace/Mile |
| | | | |

**Aches , Pains & Notes**

| Day/Date | Brief Route Info | | Walk No. 278 |
|---|---|---|---|
| | | | |

| Time Start | Time Walking | Distance | Avg Pace/Mile |
|---|---|---|---|
| | | | |

**Aches , Pains & Notes**

| Day/Date | Brief Route Info | | Walk No. 279 |
|---|---|---|---|
| | | | |

| Time Start | Time Walking | Distance | Avg Pace/Mile |
|---|---|---|---|
| | | | |

**Aches , Pains & Notes**

| Day/Date | Brief Route Info | | Walk No. 280 |
|---|---|---|---|
| | | | |

| Time Start | Time Walking | Distance | Avg Pace/Mile |
|---|---|---|---|
| | | | |

**Aches , Pains & Notes**

# SUMMARY

| Time Walking | Distance Walked | Average Pace |
|---|---|---|
| | | |

| Start Weight | Weight Now | + /- |
|---|---|---|
| | | |

# 365 DAY WALKING CHALLENGE - WEEK 41

| Day/Date | Brief Route Info | | Walk No. 281 |
|---|---|---|---|
| Time Start | Time Walking | Distance | Avg Pace/Mile |
| | | | |

**Aches , Pains & Notes**

| Day/Date | Brief Route Info | | Walk No. 282 |
|---|---|---|---|
| Time Start | Time Walking | Distance | Avg Pace/Mile |
| | | | |

**Aches , Pains & Notes**

| Day/Date | Brief Route Info | | Walk No. 283 |
|---|---|---|---|
| Time Start | Time Walking | Distance | Avg Pace/Mile |
| | | | |

**Aches , Pains & Notes**

| Day/Date | Brief Route Info | | Walk No. 284 |
|---|---|---|---|
| Time Start | Time Walking | Distance | Avg Pace/Mile |
| | | | |

**Aches , Pains & Notes**

| Day/Date | Brief Route Info | | Walk No. 285 |
|---|---|---|---|

| Time Start | Time Walking | Distance | Avg Pace/Mile |
|---|---|---|---|
| | | | |

**Aches , Pains & Notes**

| |
|---|
| |

| Day/Date | Brief Route Info | | Walk No. 286 |
|---|---|---|---|

| Time Start | Time Walking | Distance | Avg Pace/Mile |
|---|---|---|---|
| | | | |

**Aches , Pains & Notes**

| |
|---|
| |

| Day/Date | Brief Route Info | | Walk No. 287 |
|---|---|---|---|

| Time Start | Time Walking | Distance | Avg Pace/Mile |
|---|---|---|---|
| | | | |

**Aches , Pains & Notes**

| |
|---|
| |

# SUMMARY

| Time Walking | Distance Walked | Average Pace |
|---|---|---|
| | | |

| Start Weight | Weight Now | + /- |
|---|---|---|
| | | |

# 365 DAY WALKING CHALLENGE - WEEK 42

| Day/Date | Brief Route Info | | Walk No. 288 |
|---|---|---|---|
| **Time Start** | **Time Walking** | **Distance** | **Avg Pace/Mile** |
| | | | |

**Aches , Pains & Notes**

| Day/Date | Brief Route Info | | Walk No. 289 |
|---|---|---|---|
| **Time Start** | **Time Walking** | **Distance** | **Avg Pace/Mile** |
| | | | |

**Aches , Pains & Notes**

| Day/Date | Brief Route Info | | Walk No. 290 |
|---|---|---|---|
| **Time Start** | **Time Walking** | **Distance** | **Avg Pace/Mile** |
| | | | |

**Aches , Pains & Notes**

| Day/Date | Brief Route Info | | Walk No. 291 |
|---|---|---|---|
| **Time Start** | **Time Walking** | **Distance** | **Avg Pace/Mile** |
| | | | |

**Aches , Pains & Notes**

| Day/Date | Brief Route Info | | Walk No. 292 |
|---|---|---|---|

| Time Start | Time Walking | Distance | Avg Pace/Mile |
|---|---|---|---|
| | | | |

**Aches , Pains & Notes**

| | | | |
|---|---|---|---|

| Day/Date | Brief Route Info | | Walk No. 293 |
|---|---|---|---|

| Time Start | Time Walking | Distance | Avg Pace/Mile |
|---|---|---|---|
| | | | |

**Aches , Pains & Notes**

| | | | |
|---|---|---|---|

| Day/Date | Brief Route Info | | Walk No. 294 |
|---|---|---|---|

| Time Start | Time Walking | Distance | Avg Pace/Mile |
|---|---|---|---|
| | | | |

**Aches , Pains & Notes**

| | | | |
|---|---|---|---|

# SUMMARY

| Time Walking | Distance Walked | Average Pace |
|---|---|---|
| | | |

| Start Weight | Weight Now | + /- |
|---|---|---|
| | | |

# 365 DAY WALKING CHALLENGE - WEEK 43

| Day/Date | Brief Route Info | | Walk No. 295 |
|---|---|---|---|
| | | | |
| Time Start | Time Walking | Distance | Avg Pace/Mile |
| | | | |

### Aches , Pains & Notes

| Day/Date | Brief Route Info | | Walk No. 296 |
|---|---|---|---|
| | | | |
| Time Start | Time Walking | Distance | Avg Pace/Mile |
| | | | |

### Aches , Pains & Notes

| Day/Date | Brief Route Info | | Walk No. 297 |
|---|---|---|---|
| | | | |
| Time Start | Time Walking | Distance | Avg Pace/Mile |
| | | | |

### Aches , Pains & Notes

| Day/Date | Brief Route Info | | Walk No. 298 |
|---|---|---|---|
| | | | |
| Time Start | Time Walking | Distance | Avg Pace/Mile |
| | | | |

### Aches , Pains & Notes

| Day/Date | Brief Route Info | | Walk No. 299 |
|---|---|---|---|
| | | | |

| Time Start | Time Walking | Distance | Avg Pace/Mile |
|---|---|---|---|
| | | | |

**Aches , Pains & Notes**

| | | | |
|---|---|---|---|
| | | | |

| Day/Date | Brief Route Info | | Walk No. 300 |
|---|---|---|---|
| | | | |

| Time Start | Time Walking | Distance | Avg Pace/Mile |
|---|---|---|---|
| | | | |

**Aches , Pains & Notes**

| | | | |
|---|---|---|---|
| | | | |

| Day/Date | Brief Route Info | | Walk No. 301 |
|---|---|---|---|
| | | | |

| Time Start | Time Walking | Distance | Avg Pace/Mile |
|---|---|---|---|
| | | | |

**Aches , Pains & Notes**

| | | | |
|---|---|---|---|
| | | | |

# SUMMARY

| Time Walking | Distance Walked | Average Pace |
|---|---|---|
| | | |

| Start Weight | Weight Now | + /- |
|---|---|---|
| | | |

# 365 DAY WALKING CHALLENGE – WEEK 44

| Day/Date | Brief Route Info | | Walk No. 302 |
|---|---|---|---|
| | | | |

| Time Start | Time Walking | Distance | Avg Pace/Mile |
|---|---|---|---|
| | | | |

**Aches , Pains & Notes**



| Day/Date | Brief Route Info | | Walk No. 303 |
|---|---|---|---|
| | | | |

| Time Start | Time Walking | Distance | Avg Pace/Mile |
|---|---|---|---|
| | | | |

**Aches , Pains & Notes**



| Day/Date | Brief Route Info | | Walk No. 304 |
|---|---|---|---|
| | | | |

| Time Start | Time Walking | Distance | Avg Pace/Mile |
|---|---|---|---|
| | | | |

**Aches , Pains & Notes**



| Day/Date | Brief Route Info | | Walk No. 305 |
|---|---|---|---|
| | | | |

| Time Start | Time Walking | Distance | Avg Pace/Mile |
|---|---|---|---|
| | | | |

**Aches , Pains & Notes**

| Day/Date | Brief Route Info | | Walk No. 306 |
|---|---|---|---|
| | | | |

| Time Start | Time Walking | Distance | Avg Pace/Mile |
|---|---|---|---|
| | | | |

**Aches , Pains & Notes**

| |
|---|
| |

| Day/Date | Brief Route Info | | Walk No. 307 |
|---|---|---|---|
| | | | |

| Time Start | Time Walking | Distance | Avg Pace/Mile |
|---|---|---|---|
| | | | |

**Aches , Pains & Notes**

| |
|---|
| |

| Day/Date | Brief Route Info | | Walk No. 308 |
|---|---|---|---|
| | | | |

| Time Start | Time Walking | Distance | Avg Pace/Mile |
|---|---|---|---|
| | | | |

**Aches , Pains & Notes**

| |
|---|
| |

# SUMMARY

| Time Walking | Distance Walked | Average Pace |
|---|---|---|
| | | |

| Start Weight | Weight Now | + /- |
|---|---|---|
| | | |

# 365 DAY WALKING CHALLENGE - WEEK 45

| Day/Date | Brief Route Info | | Walk No. 309 |
|---|---|---|---|
| | | | |

| Time Start | Time Walking | Distance | Avg Pace/Mile |
|---|---|---|---|
| | | | |

**Aches , Pains & Notes**

| Day/Date | Brief Route Info | | Walk No. 310 |
|---|---|---|---|
| | | | |

| Time Start | Time Walking | Distance | Avg Pace/Mile |
|---|---|---|---|
| | | | |

**Aches , Pains & Notes**

| Day/Date | Brief Route Info | | Walk No. 311 |
|---|---|---|---|
| | | | |

| Time Start | Time Walking | Distance | Avg Pace/Mile |
|---|---|---|---|
| | | | |

**Aches , Pains & Notes**

| Day/Date | Brief Route Info | | Walk No. 312 |
|---|---|---|---|
| | | | |

| Time Start | Time Walking | Distance | Avg Pace/Mile |
|---|---|---|---|
| | | | |

**Aches , Pains & Notes**

| Day/Date | Brief Route Info | | Walk No. 313 |
|---|---|---|---|
| | | | |

| Time Start | Time Walking | Distance | Avg Pace/Mile |
|---|---|---|---|
| | | | |

| Aches , Pains & Notes | | | |
|---|---|---|---|
| | | | |

| Day/Date | Brief Route Info | | Walk No. 314 |
|---|---|---|---|
| | | | |

| Time Start | Time Walking | Distance | Avg Pace/Mile |
|---|---|---|---|
| | | | |

| Aches , Pains & Notes | | | |
|---|---|---|---|
| | | | |

| Day/Date | Brief Route Info | | Walk No. 315 |
|---|---|---|---|
| | | | |

| Time Start | Time Walking | Distance | Avg Pace/Mile |
|---|---|---|---|
| | | | |

| Aches , Pains & Notes | | | |
|---|---|---|---|
| | | | |

# SUMMARY

| Time Walking | Distance Walked | Average Pace |
|---|---|---|
| | | |

| Start Weight | Weight Now | + /- |
|---|---|---|
| | | |

# 365 DAY WALKING CHALLENGE - WEEK 46

| Day/Date | Brief Route Info | | Walk No. 316 |
|---|---|---|---|
| Time Start | Time Walking | Distance | Avg Pace/Mile |
| | | | |

**Aches , Pains & Notes**

| Day/Date | Brief Route Info | | Walk No. 317 |
|---|---|---|---|
| Time Start | Time Walking | Distance | Avg Pace/Mile |
| | | | |

**Aches , Pains & Notes**

| Day/Date | Brief Route Info | | Walk No. 318 |
|---|---|---|---|
| Time Start | Time Walking | Distance | Avg Pace/Mile |
| | | | |

**Aches , Pains & Notes**

| Day/Date | Brief Route Info | | Walk No. 319 |
|---|---|---|---|
| Time Start | Time Walking | Distance | Avg Pace/Mile |
| | | | |

**Aches , Pains & Notes**

| Day/Date | Brief Route Info | | Walk No. 320 |
|---|---|---|---|
| | | | |

| Time Start | Time Walking | Distance | Avg Pace/Mile |
|---|---|---|---|
| | | | |

**Aches , Pains & Notes**

| | |
|---|---|
| | |

| Day/Date | Brief Route Info | | Walk No. 321 |
|---|---|---|---|
| | | | |

| Time Start | Time Walking | Distance | Avg Pace/Mile |
|---|---|---|---|
| | | | |

**Aches , Pains & Notes**

| | |
|---|---|
| | |

| Day/Date | Brief Route Info | | Walk No. 322 |
|---|---|---|---|
| | | | |

| Time Start | Time Walking | Distance | Avg Pace/Mile |
|---|---|---|---|
| | | | |

**Aches , Pains & Notes**

| | |
|---|---|
| | |

# SUMMARY

| Time Walking | Distance Walked | Average Pace |
|---|---|---|
| | | |

| Start Weight | Weight Now | + /- |
|---|---|---|
| | | |

# 365 DAY WALKING CHALLENGE - WEEK 47

| Day/Date | Brief Route Info | | Walk No. 323 |
|---|---|---|---|

| Time Start | Time Walking | Distance | Avg Pace/Mile |
|---|---|---|---|
| | | | |

**Aches , Pains & Notes**

| Day/Date | Brief Route Info | | Walk No. 324 |
|---|---|---|---|

| Time Start | Time Walking | Distance | Avg Pace/Mile |
|---|---|---|---|
| | | | |

**Aches , Pains & Notes**

| Day/Date | Brief Route Info | | Walk No. 325 |
|---|---|---|---|

| Time Start | Time Walking | Distance | Avg Pace/Mile |
|---|---|---|---|
| | | | |

**Aches , Pains & Notes**

| Day/Date | Brief Route Info | | Walk No. 326 |
|---|---|---|---|

| Time Start | Time Walking | Distance | Avg Pace/Mile |
|---|---|---|---|
| | | | |

**Aches , Pains & Notes**

| Day/Date | Brief Route Info | | Walk No. 327 |
|---|---|---|---|
| | | | |

| Time Start | Time Walking | Distance | Avg Pace/Mile |
|---|---|---|---|
| | | | |

**Aches , Pains & Notes**

| |
|---|
| |

| Day/Date | Brief Route Info | | Walk No. 328 |
|---|---|---|---|
| | | | |

| Time Start | Time Walking | Distance | Avg Pace/Mile |
|---|---|---|---|
| | | | |

**Aches , Pains & Notes**

| |
|---|
| |

| Day/Date | Brief Route Info | | Walk No. 329 |
|---|---|---|---|
| | | | |

| Time Start | Time Walking | Distance | Avg Pace/Mile |
|---|---|---|---|
| | | | |

**Aches , Pains & Notes**

| |
|---|
| |

# SUMMARY

| Time Walking | Distance Walked | Average Pace |
|---|---|---|
| | | |

| Start Weight | Weight Now | + /- |
|---|---|---|
| | | |

# 365 DAY WALKING CHALLENGE – WEEK 48

| Day/Date | Brief Route Info | | Walk No. 330 |
|---|---|---|---|
| Time Start | Time Walking | Distance | Avg Pace/Mile |
| | | | |

**Aches , Pains & Notes**

| Day/Date | Brief Route Info | | Walk No. 331 |
|---|---|---|---|
| Time Start | Time Walking | Distance | Avg Pace/Mile |
| | | | |

**Aches , Pains & Notes**

| Day/Date | Brief Route Info | | Walk No. 332 |
|---|---|---|---|
| Time Start | Time Walking | Distance | Avg Pace/Mile |
| | | | |

**Aches , Pains & Notes**

| Day/Date | Brief Route Info | | Walk No. 333 |
|---|---|---|---|
| Time Start | Time Walking | Distance | Avg Pace/Mile |
| | | | |

**Aches , Pains & Notes**

| Day/Date | Brief Route Info | | Walk No. 334 |
|---|---|---|---|
| | | | |

| Time Start | Time Walking | Distance | Avg Pace/Mile |
|---|---|---|---|
| | | | |

**Aches , Pains & Notes**

| | | | |
|---|---|---|---|

| Day/Date | Brief Route Info | | Walk No. 335 |
|---|---|---|---|
| | | | |

| Time Start | Time Walking | Distance | Avg Pace/Mile |
|---|---|---|---|
| | | | |

**Aches , Pains & Notes**

| | | | |
|---|---|---|---|

| Day/Date | Brief Route Info | | Walk No. 336 |
|---|---|---|---|
| | | | |

| Time Start | Time Walking | Distance | Avg Pace/Mile |
|---|---|---|---|
| | | | |

**Aches , Pains & Notes**

| | | | |
|---|---|---|---|

# SUMMARY

| Time Walking | Distance Walked | Average Pace |
|---|---|---|
| | | |

| Start Weight | Weight Now | + /- |
|---|---|---|
| | | |

# 365 DAY WALKING CHALLENGE - WEEK 49

| Day/Date | Brief Route Info | | Walk No. 337 |
|---|---|---|---|
| Time Start | Time Walking | Distance | Avg Pace/Mile |
| | | | |
| Aches , Pains & Notes | | | |
| | | | |

| Day/Date | Brief Route Info | | Walk No. 338 |
|---|---|---|---|
| Time Start | Time Walking | Distance | Avg Pace/Mile |
| | | | |
| Aches , Pains & Notes | | | |
| | | | |

| Day/Date | Brief Route Info | | Walk No. 339 |
|---|---|---|---|
| Time Start | Time Walking | Distance | Avg Pace/Mile |
| | | | |
| Aches , Pains & Notes | | | |
| | | | |

| Day/Date | Brief Route Info | | Walk No. 340 |
|---|---|---|---|
| Time Start | Time Walking | Distance | Avg Pace/Mile |
| | | | |
| Aches , Pains & Notes | | | |
| | | | |

| Day/Date | Brief Route Info | | Walk No. 341 |
|---|---|---|---|
| | | | |

| Time Start | Time Walking | Distance | Avg Pace/Mile |
|---|---|---|---|
| | | | |

**Aches , Pains & Notes**

| |
|---|
| |

| Day/Date | Brief Route Info | | Walk No. 342 |
|---|---|---|---|
| | | | |

| Time Start | Time Walking | Distance | Avg Pace/Mile |
|---|---|---|---|
| | | | |

**Aches , Pains & Notes**

| |
|---|
| |

| Day/Date | Brief Route Info | | Walk No. 343 |
|---|---|---|---|
| | | | |

| Time Start | Time Walking | Distance | Avg Pace/Mile |
|---|---|---|---|
| | | | |

**Aches , Pains & Notes**

| |
|---|
| |

# SUMMARY

| Time Walking | Distance Walked | Average Pace |
|---|---|---|
| | | |

| Start Weight | Weight Now | + /- |
|---|---|---|
| | | |

# 365 DAY WALKING CHALLENGE - WEEK 50

| Day/Date | Brief Route Info | | Walk No. 344 |
|---|---|---|---|
| | | | |

| Time Start | Time Walking | Distance | Avg Pace/Mile |
|---|---|---|---|
| | | | |

**Aches , Pains & Notes**

| Day/Date | Brief Route Info | | Walk No. 345 |
|---|---|---|---|
| | | | |

| Time Start | Time Walking | Distance | Avg Pace/Mile |
|---|---|---|---|
| | | | |

**Aches , Pains & Notes**

| Day/Date | Brief Route Info | | Walk No. 346 |
|---|---|---|---|
| | | | |

| Time Start | Time Walking | Distance | Avg Pace/Mile |
|---|---|---|---|
| | | | |

**Aches , Pains & Notes**

| Day/Date | Brief Route Info | | Walk No. 347 |
|---|---|---|---|
| | | | |

| Time Start | Time Walking | Distance | Avg Pace/Mile |
|---|---|---|---|
| | | | |

**Aches , Pains & Notes**

| Day/Date | Brief Route Info | | Walk No. 348 |
|---|---|---|---|

| Time Start | Time Walking | Distance | Avg Pace/Mile |
|---|---|---|---|
| | | | |

**Aches , Pains & Notes**

| Day/Date | Brief Route Info | | Walk No. 349 |
|---|---|---|---|

| Time Start | Time Walking | Distance | Avg Pace/Mile |
|---|---|---|---|
| | | | |

**Aches , Pains & Notes**

| Day/Date | Brief Route Info | | Walk No. 350 |
|---|---|---|---|

| Time Start | Time Walking | Distance | Avg Pace/Mile |
|---|---|---|---|
| | | | |

**Aches , Pains & Notes**

# SUMMARY

| Time Walking | Distance Walked | Average Pace |
|---|---|---|
| | | |

| Start Weight | Weight Now | + /- |
|---|---|---|
| | | |

# 365 DAY WALKING CHALLENGE - WEEK 51

| Day/Date | Brief Route Info | | Walk No. 351 |
|---|---|---|---|
| Time Start | Time Walking | Distance | Avg Pace/Mile |
| | | | |

**Aches , Pains & Notes**

| Day/Date | Brief Route Info | | Walk No. 352 |
|---|---|---|---|
| Time Start | Time Walking | Distance | Avg Pace/Mile |
| | | | |

**Aches , Pains & Notes**

| Day/Date | Brief Route Info | | Walk No. 353 |
|---|---|---|---|
| Time Start | Time Walking | Distance | Avg Pace/Mile |
| | | | |

**Aches , Pains & Notes**

| Day/Date | Brief Route Info | | Walk No. 354 |
|---|---|---|---|
| Time Start | Time Walking | Distance | Avg Pace/Mile |
| | | | |

**Aches , Pains & Notes**

| Day/Date | Brief Route Info | | Walk No. 355 |
|---|---|---|---|
| | | | |

| Time Start | Time Walking | Distance | Avg Pace/Mile |
|---|---|---|---|
| | | | |

**Aches , Pains & Notes**

| Day/Date | Brief Route Info | | Walk No. 356 |
|---|---|---|---|
| | | | |

| Time Start | Time Walking | Distance | Avg Pace/Mile |
|---|---|---|---|
| | | | |

**Aches , Pains & Notes**

| Day/Date | Brief Route Info | | Walk No. 357 |
|---|---|---|---|
| | | | |

| Time Start | Time Walking | Distance | Avg Pace/Mile |
|---|---|---|---|
| | | | |

**Aches , Pains & Notes**

# SUMMARY

| Time Walking | Distance Walked | Average Pace |
|---|---|---|
| | | |

| Start Weight | Weight Now | + /- |
|---|---|---|
| | | |

# 365 DAY WALKING CHALLENGE - WEEK 52

| Day/Date | Brief Route Info | | Walk No. 358 |
|---|---|---|---|
| | | | |
| Time Start | Time Walking | Distance | Avg Pace/Mile |
| | | | |
| Aches , Pains & Notes | | | |
| | | | |

| Day/Date | Brief Route Info | | Walk No. 359 |
|---|---|---|---|
| | | | |
| Time Start | Time Walking | Distance | Avg Pace/Mile |
| | | | |
| Aches , Pains & Notes | | | |
| | | | |

| Day/Date | Brief Route Info | | Walk No. 360 |
|---|---|---|---|
| | | | |
| Time Start | Time Walking | Distance | Avg Pace/Mile |
| | | | |
| Aches , Pains & Notes | | | |
| | | | |

| Day/Date | Brief Route Info | | Walk No. 361 |
|---|---|---|---|
| | | | |
| Time Start | Time Walking | Distance | Avg Pace/Mile |
| | | | |
| Aches , Pains & Notes | | | |
| | | | |

| Day/Date | Brief Route Info | | Walk No. 362 |
|----------|------------------|---|------|

| Time Start | Time Walking | Distance | Avg Pace/Mile |
|------------|--------------|----------|---------------|
| | | | |

**Aches , Pains & Notes**

| Day/Date | Brief Route Info | | Walk No. 363 |
|----------|------------------|---|------|

| Time Start | Time Walking | Distance | Avg Pace/Mile |
|------------|--------------|----------|---------------|
| | | | |

**Aches , Pains & Notes**

| Day/Date | Brief Route Info | | Walk No. 364 |
|----------|------------------|---|------|

| Time Start | Time Walking | Distance | Avg Pace/Mile |
|------------|--------------|----------|---------------|
| | | | |

**Aches , Pains & Notes**

# SUMMARY

| Time Walking | Distance Walked | Average Pace |
|--------------|-----------------|--------------|
| | | |

| Start Weight | Weight Now | + /- |
|--------------|------------|------|
| | | |

# 365 DAY WALKING CHALLENGE - WEEK 53

| Day/Date | Brief Route Info | | Walk No. 365 |
|---|---|---|---|
| Time Start | Time Walking | Distance | Avg Pace/Mile |
| | | | |
| Aches , Pains & Notes | | | |
| | | | |

| Day/Date | Brief Route Info | | Walk No. 366 |
|---|---|---|---|
| Time Start | Time Walking | Distance | Avg Pace/Mile |
| | | | |
| Aches , Pains & Notes | | | |
| | | | |

| Day/Date | Brief Route Info | | Walk No. 367 |
|---|---|---|---|
| Time Start | Time Walking | Distance | Avg Pace/Mile |
| | | | |
| Aches , Pains & Notes | | | |
| | | | |

| Day/Date | Brief Route Info | | Walk No. 368 |
|---|---|---|---|
| Time Start | Time Walking | Distance | Avg Pace/Mile |
| | | | |
| Aches , Pains & Notes | | | |
| | | | |

| Day/Date | Brief Route Info | | Walk No. 369 |
|---|---|---|---|
| | | | |

| Time Start | Time Walking | Distance | Avg Pace/Mile |
|---|---|---|---|
| | | | |

**Aches , Pains & Notes**

| Day/Date | Brief Route Info | | Walk No. 370 |
|---|---|---|---|
| | | | |

| Time Start | Time Walking | Distance | Avg Pace/Mile |
|---|---|---|---|
| | | | |

**Aches , Pains & Notes**

| Day/Date | Brief Route Info | | Walk No. 371 |
|---|---|---|---|
| | | | |

| Time Start | Time Walking | Distance | Avg Pace/Mile |
|---|---|---|---|
| | | | |

**Aches , Pains & Notes**

# SUMMARY

| Time Walking | Distance Walked | Average Pace |
|---|---|---|
| | | |

| Start Weight | Weight Now | + /- |
|---|---|---|
| | | |

| Walk | Date | Distance | Time | Pace |
|------|------|----------|------|------|
| 1 | | | | |
| 2 | | | | |
| 3 | | | | |
| 4 | | | | |
| 5 | | | | |
| 6 | | | | |
| 7 | | | | |
| 8 | | | | |
| 9 | | | | |
| 10 | | | | |
| 11 | | | | |
| 12 | | | | |
| 13 | | | | |
| 14 | | | | |
| 15 | | | | |
| 16 | | | | |
| 17 | | | | |
| 18 | | | | |
| 19 | | | | |
| 20 | | | | |
| 21 | | | | |
| 22 | | | | |
| 23 | | | | |
| 24 | | | | |
| 25 | | | | |
| 26 | | | | |
| 27 | | | | |
| 28 | | | | |
| 29 | | | | |
| 30 | | | | |
| 31 | | | | |

| Walk | Date | Distance | Time | Pace |
|------|------|----------|------|------|
| 32 | | | | |
| 33 | | | | |
| 34 | | | | |
| 35 | | | | |
| 36 | | | | |
| 37 | | | | |
| 38 | | | | |
| 39 | | | | |
| 40 | | | | |
| 41 | | | | |
| 42 | | | | |
| 43 | | | | |
| 44 | | | | |
| 45 | | | | |
| 46 | | | | |
| 47 | | | | |
| 48 | | | | |
| 49 | | | | |
| 50 | | | | |
| 51 | | | | |
| 52 | | | | |
| 53 | | | | |
| 54 | | | | |
| 55 | | | | |
| 56 | | | | |
| 57 | | | | |
| 58 | | | | |
| 59 | | | | |
| 60 | | | | |
| 61 | | | | |
| 62 | | | | |

| Walk | Date | Distance | Time | Pace |
|------|------|----------|------|------|
| 63 | | | | |
| 64 | | | | |
| 65 | | | | |
| 66 | | | | |
| 67 | | | | |
| 68 | | | | |
| 69 | | | | |
| 70 | | | | |
| 71 | | | | |
| 72 | | | | |
| 73 | | | | |
| 74 | | | | |
| 75 | | | | |
| 76 | | | | |
| 77 | | | | |
| 78 | | | | |
| 79 | | | | |
| 80 | | | | |
| 81 | | | | |
| 82 | | | | |
| 83 | | | | |
| 84 | | | | |
| 85 | | | | |
| 86 | | | | |
| 87 | | | | |
| 88 | | | | |
| 89 | | | | |
| 90 | | | | |
| 91 | | | | |
| 92 | | | | |
| 93 | | | | |

| Walk | Date | Distance | Time | Pace |
|------|------|----------|------|------|
| 94 | | | | |
| 95 | | | | |
| 96 | | | | |
| 97 | | | | |
| 98 | | | | |
| 99 | | | | |
| 100 | | | | |
| 101 | | | | |
| 102 | | | | |
| 103 | | | | |
| 104 | | | | |
| 105 | | | | |
| 106 | | | | |
| 107 | | | | |
| 108 | | | | |
| 109 | | | | |
| 110 | | | | |
| 111 | | | | |
| 112 | | | | |
| 113 | | | | |
| 114 | | | | |
| 115 | | | | |
| 116 | | | | |
| 117 | | | | |
| 118 | | | | |
| 119 | | | | |
| 120 | | | | |
| 121 | | | | |
| 122 | | | | |
| 123 | | | | |
| 124 | | | | |

| Walk | Date | Distance | Time | Pace |
|------|------|----------|------|------|
| 125  |      |          |      |      |
| 126  |      |          |      |      |
| 127  |      |          |      |      |
| 128  |      |          |      |      |
| 129  |      |          |      |      |
| 130  |      |          |      |      |
| 131  |      |          |      |      |
| 132  |      |          |      |      |
| 133  |      |          |      |      |
| 134  |      |          |      |      |
| 135  |      |          |      |      |
| 136  |      |          |      |      |
| 137  |      |          |      |      |
| 138  |      |          |      |      |
| 139  |      |          |      |      |
| 140  |      |          |      |      |
| 141  |      |          |      |      |
| 142  |      |          |      |      |
| 143  |      |          |      |      |
| 144  |      |          |      |      |
| 145  |      |          |      |      |
| 146  |      |          |      |      |
| 147  |      |          |      |      |
| 148  |      |          |      |      |
| 149  |      |          |      |      |
| 150  |      |          |      |      |
| 151  |      |          |      |      |
| 152  |      |          |      |      |
| 153  |      |          |      |      |
| 154  |      |          |      |      |
| 155  |      |          |      |      |

| Walk | Date | Distance | Time | Pace |
|------|------|----------|------|------|
| 156 | | | | |
| 157 | | | | |
| 158 | | | | |
| 159 | | | | |
| 160 | | | | |
| 161 | | | | |
| 162 | | | | |
| 163 | | | | |
| 164 | | | | |
| 165 | | | | |
| 166 | | | | |
| 167 | | | | |
| 168 | | | | |
| 169 | | | | |
| 170 | | | | |
| 171 | | | | |
| 172 | | | | |
| 173 | | | | |
| 174 | | | | |
| 175 | | | | |
| 176 | | | | |
| 177 | | | | |
| 178 | | | | |
| 179 | | | | |
| 180 | | | | |
| 181 | | | | |
| 182 | | | | |
| 183 | | | | |
| 184 | | | | |
| 185 | | | | |
| 186 | | | | |

| Walk | Date | Distance | Time | Pace |
|------|------|----------|------|------|
| 187 | | | | |
| 188 | | | | |
| 189 | | | | |
| 190 | | | | |
| 191 | | | | |
| 192 | | | | |
| 193 | | | | |
| 194 | | | | |
| 195 | | | | |
| 196 | | | | |
| 197 | | | | |
| 198 | | | | |
| 199 | | | | |
| 200 | | | | |
| 201 | | | | |
| 202 | | | | |
| 203 | | | | |
| 204 | | | | |
| 205 | | | | |
| 206 | | | | |
| 207 | | | | |
| 208 | | | | |
| 209 | | | | |
| 210 | | | | |
| 211 | | | | |
| 212 | | | | |
| 213 | | | | |
| 214 | | | | |
| 215 | | | | |
| 216 | | | | |
| 217 | | | | |

| Walk | Date | Distance | Time | Pace |
|------|------|----------|------|------|
| 218 | | | | |
| 219 | | | | |
| 220 | | | | |
| 221 | | | | |
| 222 | | | | |
| 223 | | | | |
| 224 | | | | |
| 225 | | | | |
| 226 | | | | |
| 227 | | | | |
| 228 | | | | |
| 229 | | | | |
| 230 | | | | |
| 231 | | | | |
| 232 | | | | |
| 233 | | | | |
| 234 | | | | |
| 235 | | | | |
| 236 | | | | |
| 237 | | | | |
| 238 | | | | |
| 239 | | | | |
| 240 | | | | |
| 241 | | | | |
| 242 | | | | |
| 243 | | | | |
| 244 | | | | |
| 245 | | | | |
| 246 | | | | |
| 247 | | | | |
| 248 | | | | |

| Walk | Date | Distance | Time | Pace |
|------|------|----------|------|------|
| 249 | | | | |
| 250 | | | | |
| 251 | | | | |
| 252 | | | | |
| 253 | | | | |
| 254 | | | | |
| 255 | | | | |
| 256 | | | | |
| 257 | | | | |
| 258 | | | | |
| 259 | | | | |
| 260 | | | | |
| 261 | | | | |
| 262 | | | | |
| 263 | | | | |
| 264 | | | | |
| 265 | | | | |
| 266 | | | | |
| 267 | | | | |
| 268 | | | | |
| 269 | | | | |
| 270 | | | | |
| 271 | | | | |
| 272 | | | | |
| 273 | | | | |
| 274 | | | | |
| 275 | | | | |
| 276 | | | | |
| 277 | | | | |
| 288 | | | | |
| 289 | | | | |

| Walk | Date | Distance | Time | Pace |
|------|------|----------|------|------|
| 290 | | | | |
| 291 | | | | |
| 292 | | | | |
| 293 | | | | |
| 294 | | | | |
| 295 | | | | |
| 296 | | | | |
| 297 | | | | |
| 298 | | | | |
| 299 | | | | |
| 300 | | | | |
| 301 | | | | |
| 302 | | | | |
| 303 | | | | |
| 304 | | | | |
| 305 | | | | |
| 306 | | | | |
| 307 | | | | |
| 308 | | | | |
| 309 | | | | |
| 310 | | | | |
| 311 | | | | |
| 312 | | | | |
| 313 | | | | |
| 314 | | | | |
| 315 | | | | |
| 316 | | | | |
| 317 | | | | |
| 318 | | | | |
| 319 | | | | |
| 320 | | | | |

| Walk | Date | Distance | Time | Pace |
|------|------|----------|------|------|
| 321 | | | | |
| 322 | | | | |
| 323 | | | | |
| 324 | | | | |
| 325 | | | | |
| 326 | | | | |
| 327 | | | | |
| 328 | | | | |
| 329 | | | | |
| 330 | | | | |
| 331 | | | | |
| 332 | | | | |
| 333 | | | | |
| 334 | | | | |
| 335 | | | | |
| 336 | | | | |
| 337 | | | | |
| 338 | | | | |
| 339 | | | | |
| 340 | | | | |
| 341 | | | | |
| 342 | | | | |
| 343 | | | | |
| 344 | | | | |
| 356 | | | | |
| 346 | | | | |
| 347 | | | | |
| 348 | | | | |
| 349 | | | | |
| 350 | | | | |
| 351 | | | | |

| Walk | Date | Distance | Time | Pace |
|------|------|----------|------|------|
| 352 | | | | |
| 353 | | | | |
| 354 | | | | |
| 355 | | | | |
| 356 | | | | |
| 357 | | | | |
| 358 | | | | |
| 359 | | | | |
| 360 | | | | |
| 361 | | | | |
| 362 | | | | |
| 363 | | | | |
| 364 | | | | |
| **365** | | | | |
| 366 | | | | |
| 367 | | | | |
| 368 | | | | |
| 369 | | | | |
| 370 | | | | |
| 371 | | | | |
| | | | | |
| | | | | |
| | | | | |
| | | | | |
| | | | | |
| | | | | |
| | | | | |
| | | | | |
| | | | | |
| | | | | |

| Week | Distance | Time | Weight |
|------|----------|------|--------|
| 1 | | | |
| 2 | | | |
| 3 | | | |
| 4 | | | |
| 5 | | | |
| 6 | | | |
| 7 | | | |
| 8 | | | |
| 9 | | | |
| 10 | | | |
| 11 | | | |
| 12 | | | |
| 13 | | | |
| 14 | | | |
| 15 | | | |
| 16 | | | |
| 17 | | | |
| 18 | | | |
| 19 | | | |
| 20 | | | |
| 21 | | | |
| 22 | | | |
| 23 | | | |
| 24 | | | |
| 25 | | | |
| 26 | | | |
| 27 | | | |

| Week | Distance | Time | Weight |
|------|----------|------|--------|
| 28 | | | |
| 29 | | | |
| 30 | | | |
| 31 | | | |
| 32 | | | |
| 33 | | | |
| 34 | | | |
| 35 | | | |
| 36 | | | |
| 37 | | | |
| 38 | | | |
| 39 | | | |
| 40 | | | |
| 41 | | | |
| 42 | | | |
| 43 | | | |
| 44 | | | |
| 45 | | | |
| 46 | | | |
| 47 | | | |
| 48 | | | |
| 49 | | | |
| 50 | | | |
| 51 | | | |
| 52 | | | |
| 53 | | | |
| 54 | | | |

| Month | Distance | Time | Weight |
|---|---|---|---|
|  |  |  |  |
|  |  |  |  |
|  |  |  |  |
|  |  |  |  |
|  |  |  |  |
|  |  |  |  |
|  |  |  |  |
|  |  |  |  |
|  |  |  |  |
|  |  |  |  |
|  |  |  |  |
|  |  |  |  |
| Totals |  |  |  |

# 365
## ONE YEAR WALKING CHALLENGE

## ONE YEAR SUMMARY

| TOTAL MILES | WEIGHT START | WEIGHT FINISH | WEIGHT LOST |
|---|---|---|---|
|  |  |  |  |

Made in the USA
Monee, IL
10 January 2025

76508081R10070